Moths, Butterflies, Other Insects, and Spiders

Science in Art, Song, and Play

Rhonda Vansant, Ed.D.

Barbara L. Dondiego, M.Ed.

Illustrations by

Claire Kalish

Science in Every Sense

TAB Books
Division of McGraw-Hill, Inc.
New York San Francisco Washington, D.C. Auckland Bogotá Caracas Lisbon London Madrid
Mexico City Milan Montreal New Delhi San Juan Singapore Sydney Tokyo Toronto

This book is printed on recycled paper containing a minimum of 50% total recycled fiber with 15% postconsumer de-inked fiber.

pbk   2 3 4 5 6 7 8 9 BBC/BBC 9 9 8 7 6 5
hc   2 3 4 5 6 7 8 9 BBC/BBC 9 9 8 7 6 5

Library of Congress Cataloging-in-Publication Data
Vansant, Rhonda.
      Moths, butterflies, insects, and spiders : science in art, song,
and play / by Rhonda Vansant, Barbara L. Dondiego ; illustrated by
Claire Kalish.
         p.   cm.
      Includes index.
      ISBN 0-07-017907-7 (h)   ISBN 0-07-017906-9 (p)
      1. Insects—Study and teaching (Early childhood) 2. Spiders—
Study and teaching (Early childhood) 3. Insects—Study and
teaching—Activity programs.   4. Spiders—Study and teaching—
Activity programs.   I. Dondiego, Barbara L.   II. Kalish, Clarie.
III. Title.
QL468.5.V36   1995   94-45011
372.3'57—dc20   CIP

Acquisitions editor: Kimberly Tabor
Editorial team: Jeanette R. Shearer, Book Editor
                        David M. McCandless, Managing Editor
                        Joanne M. Slike, Executive Editor
                        Joann Woy, Indexer
Production team: Katherine G. Brown, Director
                        Wanda S. Ditch, Desktop Operator
                        Janice Stottlemyer, Computer Artist
Design team: Jaclyn J. Boone, Designer
                        Kathryn Stefanski, Associate Designer

0179077
SIES

Moths,
Butterflies,
Other Insects,
and Spiders

Other Books by Barbara Dondiego

After School Crafts

Crafts for Kids: A Month-by-Month Idea Book, 2nd edition

Year-Round Crafts for Kids

Cats, Dogs, and Classroom Pets

About the Authors

Barbara Dondiego holds a master's degree in education from the University of Virginia, and a bachelor of science degree in foods and nutrition from Oregon State University. She is a state-certified educational consultant who conducts regular workshops for preschool teachers. Barbara is author of TAB's *Crafts for Kids: A Month-by-Month Idea Book, Year-Round Crafts for Kids*, and *After-School Crafts*.

Rhonda Vansant has a doctorate of education from Vanderbilt University, has taught classes at both the elementary and college levels, and serves as an educational consultant. She conducts workshops and gives conference presentations on methodologies for teaching young children. Rhonda is also a member of the National Association for the Education of Young Children and the Association of Childhood Education International.

Dedication

To my mother, who demonstrated through her own life
the love and care of all living things and instilled in me
a reverence for nature.
With love,
Rhonda

To Mike and Nancy, who share with each other their love
for living things.
With love,
Mom

Acknowledgments

A special thank-you goes to Kim Tabor, Editor-in-Chief of
TAB /McGraw-Hill, for her guidance and encouragement throughout
the conception of this series. Her advice was invaluable.
We would also like to thank Jeanette Shearer, David McCandless,
Joanne Slike, Joann Woy, Katherine Brown, Wanda Ditch,
Janice Stottlemyer, Jackie Boone, and Kathryn Stefanski of
TAB/McGraw-Hill for their hard work and dedication.

Contents

A Letter to Teachers

Dear Teachers,

Maybe you're one of many educators who feels a certain anxiety about teaching science. Perhaps your science courses in school and college were stressful as you plodded through specific experiments, tried to memorize the periodic table, and tried to understand phenomena without the opportunity to build concepts first. You probably have forgotten much of the science instruction because much of it went only in short-term memory and had no direct link to what you were encountering in your world at that time. Perhaps you never had a role model who felt a passion about loving and caring for the world—a role model who would dare to teach you "how" to learn rather than "what" to learn.

Whether you place yourself in this category or were blessed with good role models who instilled in you a zeal for learning science, we hope this book will contribute to meaningful and enjoyable science instruction in your class.

Because we embrace the definition that science for young children is studying and exploring our world, we strongly feel that science should be the focus of an Early Childhood curriculum. Although this is a science book, it is indeed a book about life and learning. It is designed to serve as a framework for a thematic study. Within this framework, you can add your own literature, math experiences, writing experiences and other activities within content areas. The format of this book allows your teaching and learning experiences to flow naturally together in an integrated way.

We hope that you will find this to be a comfortable format for teaching science and that you will enjoy, with your students, the journey of discovery. Perhaps you will be one who inspires this generation of children to find joy and excitement in learning about the wonders that surround us.

Sincerely,

Rhonda Vansant

Barbara L. Dowling

A Letter to Parents

Dear Parents,

Generations of children have grown up feeling that science was too difficult, too stressful. Many children have avoided science and ranked it among their least favorite subjects.

How wonderful to think that we might change that attitude for the current generation. We the authors view science as studying and exploring our world in ways that are appropriate for the learner's stage of development. Children explore the world quite naturally, and we want to build upon the natural inclinations of children by guiding their explorations and nurturing their curiosity. When children see their ice cream melt, they have an opportunity to learn about their world. When children feel the wind blow, they are discovering information about their world. We do not have to search for expensive equipment to teach science to young children; we simply need to take advantage of everything that is already around us.

One of the most precious gifts we can give our children is a love of learning. We hope you will find ways to use this book with your own children as well as with groups of children in various organizations. It is our hope that you may nurture your children's natural wonder and curiosity about our world and that the dream that this generation will come to love, understand, and cherish this world will come true.

Sincerely,

Rhonda Vansant

Introduction

Insects and spiders have always intrigued children. Some children, however, have mistakenly learned that these animals are all mere nuisances, and they never have opportunities to observe, study, and learn to appreciate how these animals live and carry out their purposes in life. As children discover how insects and spiders affect their world, they develop a respect for living things. Studying insects and spiders fosters children's natural curiosity about the world around them and encourages them to use their five senses.

Building concepts

Studying animals allows children to experience real objects or living things. This is called a *concrete experience*. If the topic of study is spiders, for example, we should provide children with opportunities to see and investigate real spiders. When we do so, we are *building a concept*. Concepts are the foundation for subsequent learning. After children experience reality, they can then make models or re-create the experience in a variety of ways. Models and pictures are called *semi-concrete representations*. Words that we attach to these experiences are called *symbolic representations*. The word *butterfly* written in a book symbolizes a living and breathing animal that we experience many times in our lives. Giving children opportunities to experience real living and nonliving things helps them develop concepts that, in turn, give meaning to the written and spoken word.

Moths, Butterflies, Other Insects, and Spiders provides opportunities for children to build concepts by introducing them to a variety of insects and spiders. Children can observe these animals on nature walks or while keeping them in the classroom for study. The book is written as a cross-curricular guide to enable parents and teachers to teach children about these animals all day long if desired! Each animal study includes some or all of the following:

☐ **Art** Creating lifelike models

☐ **Creative drama** Acting, pretending

☐ **Music and dancing** Singing songs and moving creatively

☐ **Informational books** Finding facts

☐ **Research** Using the five senses to discover information; reading and looking at pictures; talking to people

☐ **Writing** Preparing factual reports or creating essays, poems, or stories to express thoughts and emotions

☐ **Cooking** Using a variety of skills to create treats

☐ **Mathematics** Measuring, counting

Each chapter in this book presents factual information you can read aloud to the children. You might want the children to sit on the floor near you while you share this information. If you keep a chart of important words for the children's future writing, place it nearby so that you can add words throughout your reading and discussion time.

Teaching children science

For young children, science should not be a set of experiments with specific steps that must be followed. It should involve a very natural discovery of their world through real experiences, creative art, literature, drama, music, writing, reading, and play. Whenever we teach children to use their five senses, we are teaching science. Whenever we provide opportunities for exploration and discovery, we are teaching science. Whenever we help children get to know the world around them, we are teaching science. Whenever we teach children to love and care for the world, we are teaching science.

The following science skills are appropriate for instruction with young children. You will be helping children use these skills as you pursue your study.

1. *Observing* Using any of the five senses to become aware of objects
2. *Following directions* Listening to or reading step-by-step directions and carrying them out
3. *Classifying* Arranging objects or information in groups according to some method
4. *Creating models* Portraying information through multisensory representations
5. *Manipulating materials* Handling materials safely and effectively
6. *Measuring* Making quantitative observations (time, temperature, weight, length, etc.)
7. *Using numbers* Applying mathematical rules
8. *Asking questions* Verbally demonstrating curiosity
9. *Finding information* Locating words, pictures, or numbers
10. *Making predictions* Suggesting what may happen (Predictions should come after children have some experiences with the topic. Predictions should be based on previously gathered data.)
11. *Designing investigations* Coming up with a plan to find out information or answers to questions
12. *Communicating or recording information* Communicating or recording information by the following:
    * talking to the teacher and/or other children
    * playing with theme related props
    * drawing pictures
    * labeling
    * making diagrams
    * making graphs
    * writing (descriptive in learning logs or narrative)
    * making photographs with a camera
    * recording on audio or videotape
13. *Drawing conclusions* Coming to various conclusions based on their stage of cognitive growth and their prior experiences
14. *Applying knowledge* Finding ways to use what is learned

About this book

Each chapter starts with a science goal to guide the parents and teachers. The goal is followed by ideas on how to plan for the activities, as well as lists of visual aids and related words that can be used for discussion.

Safety symbols, or icons, have been placed in the text to alert parents and teachers about activities that require supervision or other precautions.

 Scissors

 Adult supervision

Discussion Ideas, Activity Ideas, and Science Skills are also indicated by symbols in the text:

 Discussion Ideas includes questions for discussion that the teacher can ask the children.

 Activity Ideas incorporates multicurricular activities such as art, music, and drama that can easily by planned ahead of time and implemented throughout the study.

 Science Skills details exactly what that child will learn by performing the activity.

Caterpillar Corner and Let's Create are interspersed throughout the text. Caterpillar Corner contains interesting tidbits of information to be passed along verbally to the children or instructional information for the teacher or parent. Let's Create includes directions and simple patterns so the children can build actual models of the animals being studied. Children personify objects quite naturally; they enjoy giving their models names and personalities as they use them in a variety of ways. All of the Let's Create ideas can be embellished with a child's creative thoughts of how an animal might look or behave. The models can then be used in preplanned activities as well as spontaneous play.

A final word

For parents and teachers, every moment is an opportunity to teach science. By using this book, children will experience real animals, create models of animals, hear and read stories about them, act out animal plays, and truly come to know animals in many ways. As each child moves from the real to the semi-concrete to the symbolic, he or she gains a true understanding of insects and spiders in the world. We hope the children enjoy studying these creatures by performing the activities in this book. More importantly, we hope that their sensitivity to the living creatures in their world will be enhanced.

chapter **1**

INSECTS

Science goals
To help children become aware of what insects are like, how they grow, what they do, and their purpose in the world

Teacher/Parent planning
You might want to order a set of plastic insects from a school supply store. Plastic insects are very realistic and safe for the children to play with and hold. You might purchase or create a small insect box to keep an insect in for a short time while children look at it. (See Let's Create an Insect Box below.) Have magnifying glasses available for the children to use. Magnifying insect viewers are wonderful. The viewer is a clear, plastic cup with a lid that magnifies whatever is in the cup.

You can also buy an ant farm. Borrow books from the library. Arrange for guest speakers to come. Prepare to write words about insects on a large sheet of chart paper.

Materials needed for discussion and activities
- ☐ Informational books
- ☐ Insect box
- ☐ Chart paper
- ☐ Large jar for ants
- ☐ Construction paper
- ☐ Plastic insect collection or pictures
- ☐ Easel and paints
- ☐ Magnifying glasses
- ☐ Magnifying insect viewer
- ☐ Plastic insect collection ant farm (optional)

Related words

insect An animal that has six legs, a body divided into three different parts, and a tough, shell-like covering

metamorphosis Changes in the appearance, functions, and habits of an animal during its life

hibernate To sleep and remain inactive throughout the winter

Let's Create an Insect Box

Manipulating materials including a cylinder; following directions
Prepare for an outdoor nature walk by creating an insect box for collecting specimens (Fig. 1-1). Nylon screening can be cut with scissors to create a window. Plaster of Paris seals the screen at the bottom, and provides a base for insect climbing sticks.

■ **1-1** *Let's create an Insect Box.*

What you need
- ☐ Cylinder-shaped oatmeal cereal box with a lid (or a similar container)
- ☐ Construction paper
- ☐ White glue
- ☐ Scissors
- ☐ Markers or crayons
- ☐ Nylon window screening (can be purchased from a hardware store)
- ☐ Heavy tape such as packing tape or duct tape
- ☐ Plaster of Paris (can be purchased from a hardware store)
- ☐ Water
- ☐ Disposable bowl for mixing plaster
- ☐ Disposable spoon or craft stick for mixing plaster
- ☐ Twigs, moss, leaves, or similar natural items
- ☐ Yarn

Directions
1. Glue construction paper on the outside of your oatmeal box, covering it completely, as shown in Fig. 1-2. Let the glue dry.

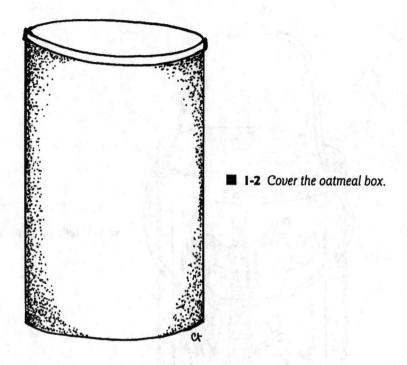

■ **I-2** *Cover the oatmeal box.*

2. Use scissors to cut a large window in the side of the box, as shown in Fig. 1-3.
3. Cut a piece of nylon screen. It should be tall enough to reach from the top of the box to the bottom, and wide enough to extend 1½ inches past the window on each side, as shown in Fig. 1-4.
4. Place the screen inside the box to cover the window. Seal the side edges of the screen with tape.

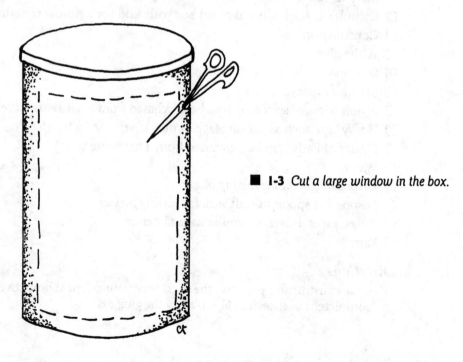

■ **I-3** *Cut a large window in the box.*

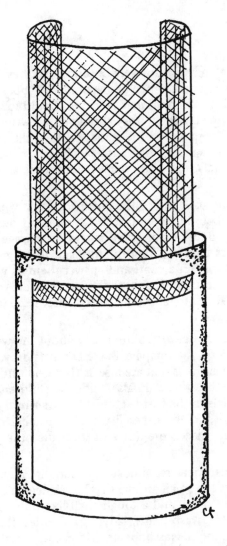

■ **I-4** *Place the screen inside the box.*

5. To make the box brighter inside, line the inside back of it with yellow or white paper.

6. Put 1 cup Plaster of Paris in a disposable bowl. Stir in water until the plaster is as thick as cake batter. Pour the plaster into the bottom of the insect cage, smoothing it against the bottom edge of the screen window. Be careful not to get plaster on the window itself!

7. Immediately insert the end of a twig in the plaster. Add leaves and moss if you wish. Let the plaster become firm. The drying process takes about 20 minutes.

8. Decorate the outside of the box with insect stickers, drawings, or pictures of insects.

 9. After the insect box dries overnight, poke a hole through both sides near the top. Thread a piece of yarn through both holes, and tie the ends together, as shown in Fig. 1-1.

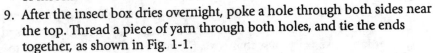

Nature walk

 Observing; asking questions

Begin this unit of study by taking a nature walk outdoors. So they can draw, give each child a piece of paper and a pencil or crayon. (A clipboard is wonderful for nature walks.) Tell the children that everyone should look for any kind of animal. When they see an animal, they should either write its name or draw a picture of it on their paper. As the leader of the walk, be sure to guide them in noticing small creatures like ants, ladybugs, or inchworms. Hopefully, by the end of the walk, they should have listed some animals like dog, bird, ant, butterfly, fly, or bee.

Take insect boxes along on the walk and collect any insects that you can. Let the children observe and talk about these insects for an hour or so. Have them draw the insects that you discuss on their papers. Encourage the children to ask questions. You can answer their questions at this time, or you might want to list the questions on a chart and answer them as you move through the study. Be sure to return the insects to the places where you found them. Let the children go with you to return the insects. They need to see this kind of good role modeling.

When you get back to the room, let the children talk about the words and pictures thcy wrote and drew on their papers. Make two lists on your chart paper. On one side, write the animals that are insects (but don't title the list yet). On the other side, write the other animals. Guide the children in a discussion about how the animals in the first list are alike. Later in the discussion, label this list "Insects" and the other list could be labeled "Other Animals." Talk about how the insects are different from the other animals you saw on the walk.

Insects are fascinating animals. There are almost a million different kinds of insects in the world. An insect is a small animal that has six legs, a body that is divided into three different parts, and a tough shell-like outer covering. Some kinds of insects are bees, wasps, ants, ladybugs, fireflies, fleas, ticks, house flies, dragonflies, mosquitoes, grasshoppers, crickets, termites, roaches, beetles, moths, and butterflies.

 Talking about insects

 Communicating information; finding information

"Let's talk about some insects that you have seen." Encourage the children to talk about insects they have seen outdoors or in their home or school. List these insects on the chart or write them on the chalkboard. If you have encyclopedias available, find each of these insects and let the children look at the pictures.

Give the children time to look through the informational books. Use the pictures to point out examples as you read the following:

Insects begin their lives as eggs. They go through stages of development and change in various ways until they look like the insect we are used to seeing. Many insects live less than a year, but some insects can live up to 50 years.

We have a skeleton inside our bodies. Insects have a skeleton on the outside of their bodies. This skeleton is called an *exoskeleton*. It protects the inside of the insect. Our bones grow with us, but the exoskeleton does not grow. It gets too tight for the insect, and it comes off. A new exoskeleton forms under the old one so that after the old one comes off, the new one is able to stretch because it is soft for a while. Once an insect becomes an adult, it does not need to grow a new skeleton.

An insect has three body parts: the head, the thorax, and the abdomen. The head is made up of mouth parts, eyes, and antennae. The mouth parts are structures the insect uses to feed itself. Different insects have different mouth parts, but there are two main types: one is used for chewing and one is used for sucking. Insects that chew have jaws lined with teeth. They also have two lips. Insects that suck their food might have a long beak or a tube.

Most insects have two eyes. Their eyes are fascinating because they are made up of many lenses. All the lenses help combine things to form a complete picture for the insect. Insects do not have eyelids, so their eyes are open all the time.

Most insects have two *antennae* between their eyes. They use their antennae to feel and smell. Some insects use their antennae to taste and hear. (Most insects do not have ears.) Insects use their sense of smell to search for food and find their way around. Insects have brains. Their brains receive and send messages from the eyes and antennae to the body. Insects have tiny hairs all over their bodies. These hairs are very sensitive for touching objects and to the air movement around the insect. If you try to get close to a fly, it can feel the air movement and will fly off before you can touch it.

The middle section of an insect's body is called the *thorax*. The six legs are connected to the thorax. Each leg has joints that help it move. Insects have different kinds of legs. Some legs are made for swimming, some for digging, some for jumping, some for holding on, and some for cleaning.

Most insects have wings. Some insects have two wings that are connected to the thorax. Some insects have four wings.

The last section of an insect's body is called the *abdomen*. The abdomen contains organs that digest food, helps produce babies, and gets rid of waste products. Did you know that insects have a stomach and an intestine?

Insects have a heart, which pumps blood throughout the inside of the insect's body. An insect's blood is not red like ours, but can be yellowish, greenish, or clear. Insects do not have veins like we do; their blood fills their whole body.

An insect breathes air through tiny holes along the sides of its body called *spiracles*. Oxygen from the air is then carried to all the parts of the body and carbon dioxide is carried away.

Have you ever seen an ant carrying an object bigger than it is? Well, insects have muscles that help them to carry objects or food, jump, dig, fly, and do many other things. Many insects have more muscles than a person does, but, of course, the muscles are much smaller.

☞ *Looking at insects*

🔍 *Classifying; finding information; recording information*
If you have a set of plastic insects, let the children hold and look at them. Let the children use reference books to find the names of each kind and to learn

more about them. Pass out index cards or something similar on which the children can write the names of the insects. Then, on a small table, display the index cards and lay the insects on top of the corresponding cards. Older children can write some information on the card as well as the insect's name. You can invent games with the cards and insects. For instance, you might guide the children in classifying the insects as big or little, long or short, and one color or more than one color.

You can also use pictures of insects or keep some dead insects that you have found in magnifying insect viewers. Please avoid having children collect insects and pinning them to a board. This practice does not encourage good scientific approaches.

Ant

 Let's visit ants

Observing

Take your children outdoors to visit some ants. Before going, talk to them about safely watching ants: not stepping on the ants, not letting the ants get on them, not touching ants with their hands. Let a few children at a time watch the ants. Talk about what the ants look like. Talk about what the ants are doing. Ask the children to listen carefully. "Do you hear anything?" "Are the ants making any sounds?" "How do you think they talk to one another?"

You might want to collect some of the ants to take back to the room. A jar with dirt in it and a lid with a few tiny air holes is fine to keep the ants in for a short time. An open jar can be put in a shallow container of water because ants do not go into water. Put a little piece of a wet sponge in the jar so the ants can drink water from it. Give them some food like seeds, bread, or sweets. Keep the jar in a dark place some of the time, so the ants feel like they are underground.

An ant is one of the most common insects that we see. Like us, it is a living thing. It can walk and run, see and feel, push and pull, pick up things, and carry things. It eats, works, and builds a home. Its body has three parts: the head, the thorax, and the abdomen. Ants like to live with many other ants in a home called a *colony*. A colony can have 10 ants, 100 ants, or a million ants.

The mother is called the *queen*, and she lays the eggs. Ants live on land. They live in most parts of the world except where it is very cold. Ants usually live in underground tunnels, in mounds on top of the ground, under rocks, inside trees, or inside hollow parts of other plants.

Ants can be brown, black, red, yellow, green, purple, or blue. Different kinds of ants are different sizes. The smallest kind of ant is about 1/10 of a centimeter long. The largest kind of ant is more than 1 inch long.

Even though ants are very small, they are very strong. They can carry objects that weigh 10 times more than they do.

In the ant's head are the ant's brain, mouth, eyes, and antennae. Its mouth is made up of a tongue and jaws. One set of jaws move from side to side. These jaws are called *mandibles*. They are used to get food, carry the young ants, and fight enemies. Mandibles can also be used to dig or cut through wood. Ants have another set of jaws that chew food into small pieces. The ant's tongue laps up the food, puts it into a small pouch near the mouth where muscles squeeze out the liquid, and spits out the rest of the food. Ants eat other insects, fruits, and parts of plants. The ant's antennae are used for smelling and touching. When an ant wants food from another ant, it taps on the other ant's head with its antennae. This action is one way that ants communicate with each other.

> *Caterpillar corner* *The inner set of jaws is called* maxillae. *Each maxilla has a comb that is made up of tiny hairs. The ant uses this comb to clean its antennae.*

Like all insects, ants have six legs that are part of the thorax. Ants use their legs and feet to touch, grasp, push, and pull. Ants have two hooked claws on each foot. These claws help the ant climb trees and walk all around plants and objects. These claws help the ant dig up the dirt to make tunnels underground.

Some ants have wings on their thorax. These ants are like royalty. They are the young princes and princesses. A princess ant has thin, lacy wings. When it is time for her to become a queen ant, she takes off her wings, and then she starts a home and family.

In the third part of the ant's body, the abdomen, the ant has two stomachs. The smaller stomach is for digesting its own food. The larger one is used for carrying food for other ants. When one ant wants food from another ant, it taps the other one's head with its feelers. The ants put their mouths together and one brings up some nectar from its larger stomach and passes it into the other ant's mouth.

Ants have a stinger that can put out poison at the end of its body. Ants use the stinger to protect themselves from other animals or people.

Ants like to live together in their colony, which has many rooms, where they build various kinds of nests. Ants build rooms for the babies, rooms to store food, and rooms to store "trash" until it can be taken out to the "town dump." (Ants have a special place for their "dump.") The queen has a special room of her own. Ants even have their own cemeteries where they bury dead ants. The ants in the colony are divided into groups. The queen is like the mother; she lays eggs throughout her life. The workers are all females and take care of the queen, their home, and the baby ants, and they find food. In winter, ants hibernate in a deep room away from the cold. They stay huddled together in a ball to keep warm.

Ants cannot talk like we do. They communicate with each other by tapping their antennae on each other, the walls of plants, or leaf nests. Some ants have a part of their body that can buzz or squeak. Some ants give off a chemical from their bodies. If an ant finds food, it can leave a chemical trail as it walks back to the nest so that other ants can smell the chemical and follow the trail back to the food.

> *Caterpillar corner* *Male ants do not work. Their function is to mate, and then they die within a short time.*

There are many kinds of ants, and they eat all kinds of foods. Army ants travel in large groups like armies. They eat other insects, like termites. Leaf-cutting ants, also called parasol ants, cut leaves and make underground gardens. They grow mushrooms in their garden. Harvester ants collect seeds and store them in special chambers in the nest. Harvester ants make hills or mounds for their homes. Honey ants gather honeydew from insects and plants and store it in their nests. Janitor ants make their nests in hollow tree twigs. The soldier janitor ant has a strangely shaped head. See if you can find a picture of this kind of ant. Pavement ants live under a sidewalk. Carpenter ants build their nests in rotting wood.

Let's Create a Carpenter Ant

 Learning about the anatomy of a carpenter ant by drawing a model; using reference material to find out about ants
A carpenter ant has a head, thorax, and abdomen just like other insects. Draw or construct a carpenter ant. Then create a place for it to live.

What you need
☐ Book about ants
☐ Construction paper or drawing paper
☐ Pencil
☐ Crayons
☐ Scissors
☐ White glue

Directions
1. Find out what carpenter ants look like by observing live ones and then by reading about them in a book or two.
 2. Use the pattern in Fig. 1-5 to draw an ant's body. Add legs, eyes, antennae, and other parts either by drawing and coloring them, or by cutting them out of construction paper and gluing them to the body.
3. Draw or construct a place for your carpenter ant to live.

■ **1-5** *The pattern for the Carpenter Ant.*

☞ Let's draw an ant home

⚲ Creating models

Help children look up the word *ant* in the encyclopedia. Try to find pictures of ant homes with chambers. You should also look for types of homes in other informational books. Talk about the many types of ant homes.

Give each child a piece of white construction paper. Ask him or her to draw a home for ants and to draw the ants in the different chambers. Think of ways to give the picture some reality. For example, if a child draws an anthill, let him or her spread a thin layer of glue on the ant nest (except for the chambers—leave them plain) and sprinkle dirt over the glue. The picture will have the effect of a real ant home. Give the children an opportunity to share their creations with one another.

Ants can be helpful because they eat some kinds of insects that hurt farmers' crops. By building their nests underground, they help loosen up the soil for planting time. But ants also do things that are not helpful. They can also destroy farmers' crops. They can sting people, which is very painful.

☞ What food do ants like best?

⚲ Making predictions; designing investigations

Ask the children to think of a way to find out which of three foods ants like best. They might, for example, choose to test sugar, bread crumbs, and salt. You might want to divide the children into groups of three or four.

Give the children plenty of time to brainstorm ideas, then write the ideas on a chalkboard or a chart. Discuss each idea and make modifications so that each group can conduct their own investigation. Let the children make predictions if they want, but remember that in science we do not guess; we make predictions based on prior knowledge. The following is an example of a possible plan that would work:

Use a large, plastic dinner plate. On the plate, put 1 teaspoon of sugar, 1 teaspoon of bread crumbs, and 1 teaspoon of salt. Take the plate outside to an anthill. Lay it beside the anthill and watch it for 20 minutes. See which food the ants come to first. You can also see which food they come to more often. At the end of the 20 minutes, try to tell which food the ants ate more of by seeing what food is left. Another plan might look like the following:

Collect some ants in a large jar. On a small piece of foil (small enough that it fits into the jar), put ⅛ teaspoon of birdseed, flour, and dry Jello. Leave it in the jar for one hour. In the beginning, wait to see which food the ants come to first. Later, return to see which food the ants preferred.

> ### *Caterpillar corner* Controlling variables is important in science.
> *Be sure the children use the same amount of all the ingredients they choose to test. Also, remember that predictions should be based on knowledge we have gained through prior experiences. Avoid using the word* guess *in science. Guessing is arriving at a conclusion with little or no evidence.*

Ladybug

☞ *Let's visit a ladybug*

🔍 *Observing*

If possible, bring a real ladybug to class for the children to see. Keep it in an insect box or a jar for a short time, then release it back to nature. Talk to the children about the harm of keeping something in captivity and the need for creatures to be free so that they can carry out their purposes in life. As you observe the ladybug, talk about its size, color, and what it is doing.

Find *ladybug* in the encyclopedia and in other informational books. Let the children look at the pictures. Have them read the information or read it to them.

A ladybug is a pretty insect. Most ladybugs are red with black spots, though there are many kinds of ladybugs. Some ladybugs are yellow with black spots, black with yellow spots, or red with yellow spots. The common ladybug has seven spots. Like all insects, ladybugs have six legs and three body parts. Did you know that a ladybug has two pairs of wings? The first pair on the outside are hard. They protect the second pair of wings underneath which are transparent (clear in color). The legs and the wings are attached to the middle part of the ladybug's body.

☞ *Painting*

🔍 *Recording information*

At the easel, let children paint pictures of ladybugs. They can paint a common ladybug or one of the other color combinations about which you read. Have pictures, books, and real ladybugs, if possible, for the children to refer to as they paint.

A ladybug's favorite food is another kind of insect called an *aphid*. Aphids are very tiny insects that drink juices from plants. They are harmful to plants. Ladybugs eat the aphids, so ladybugs are helpful to plants in this way.

A mother ladybug lays her small, yellow eggs on a leaf that has many aphids on it. When the eggs hatch, tiny black larvae come out. These larvae eat the aphids. The baby larva eats and grows until it is time for it to become a grownup ladybug, when it attaches itself to a leaf. The larva's old skin comes off and the larva's new skin becomes a hard, dry shell in which the grownup ladybug forms. In about a week, the ladybug comes out of this shell. It is kind of wet and its body is yellow. After a while, the wings on the outside become hard and turn another color with some spots.

Some ladybugs hibernate during cold winter months. They might stay in a hollow place in a tree or under a pile of leaves or in between rocks. They snuggle up together and take a long nap until warm weather comes again.

Let's Create a Ladybug Beetle Puppet

Learning the basic anatomy of all beetles by creating a model; manipulating materials; using reference material to learn about and create a ladybug environment

Although the ladybug looks like half a ball, it has a head, thorax, and abdomen like all beetles do. It also has four wings. Two hard and brightly colored front wings cover most of the abdomen. These wings lift up to expose two filmy hind wings with which the ladybug flies. Create a ladybug puppet with three paper plates.

What you need

☐ Three 9-inch paper plates
☐ Scissors
☐ White glue
☐ Crayons
☐ Tissue paper
☐ Markers
☐ Stapler
☐ Construction paper
☐ Two glue-on movable eyes, size 7 mm

Directions

1. Find some books in your library about real ladybug beetles. As you create your model, try to make it look like a real beetle (Fig. 1-6).

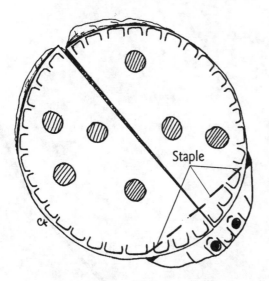

Staple

■ **1-6** *The Ladybug Beetle Puppet. Staple the front wings onto the thorax.*

2. Trace and cut out the ladybug body pattern in Fig. 1-7. Lay it on two of the paper plates and cut the pattern out of both plates.

3. Draw lines across the ladybug body to show the head, the thorax, and the abdomen. Color the entire body with crayons.

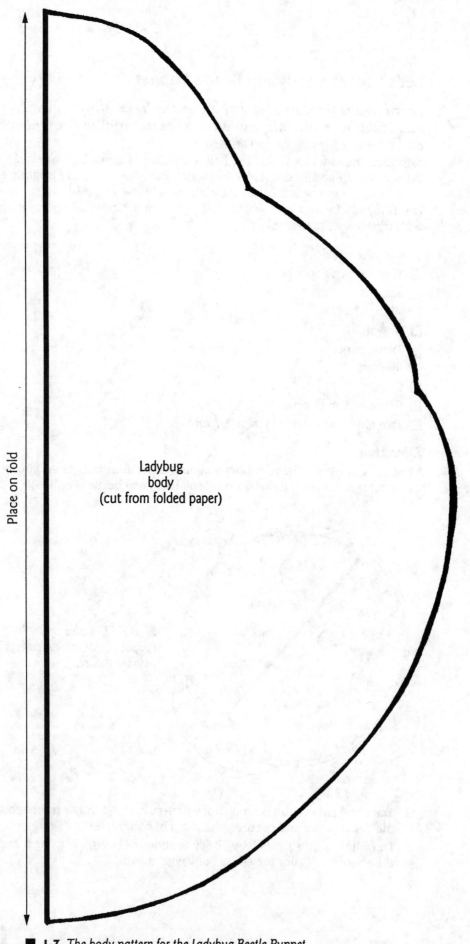

Place on fold

Ladybug
body
(cut from folded paper)

■ **I-7** *The body pattern for the Ladybug Beetle Puppet.*

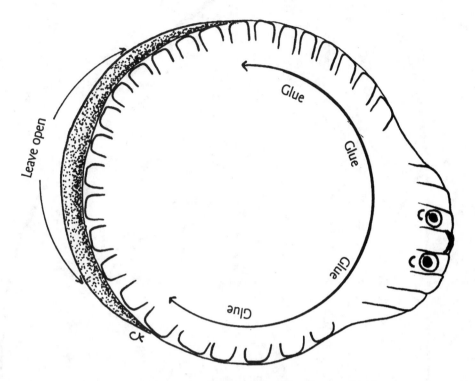

■ **I-8** *Glue the two plates together leaving an opening for your hand.*

4. Glue the two plates together around the edges as shown in Fig. 1-8, but leave the end of the abdomen open. Let the glue dry. You can put your hand into the space created by leaving one end open.

5. Fold the third paper plate in half. Cut on the fold to create two front wings. Color the wings to look like a real ladybug. Add spots with a marker or glue paper circles onto the colored wings.

6. Use the pattern in Fig. 1-9 to trace two hind wings onto tissue paper. Cut them out. Glue one end of them on top of the thorax, as shown in Fig. 1-10.

7. Staple the two front wings onto the thorax, as shown in Fig. 1-6. Glue two wiggle eyes onto the head.

8. To make six legs, cut out a construction paper 7-×-1½-inch rectangle. Follow the diagram in Fig. 1-11 to cut slits on each end of the rectangle, creating six legs. Bend the legs up or down, and then glue them under the thorax (Fig. 1-12).

9. Put your hand in your beetle to make it fly.

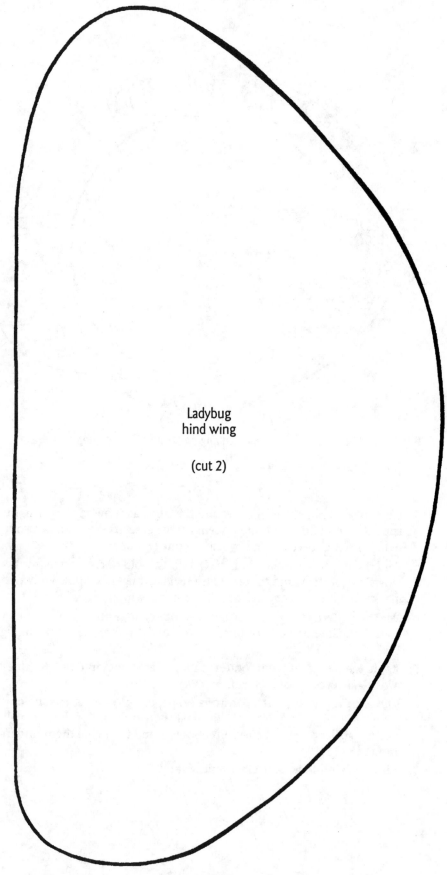

Ladybug
hind wing

(cut 2)

■ **I-9** *The hind wing pattern for the Ladybug Beetle.*

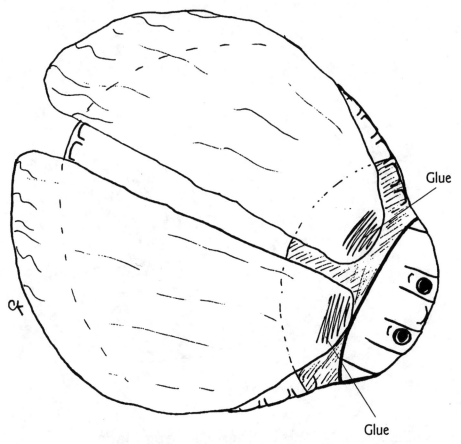

Glue

Glue

■ **1-10** *Glue the tissue paper hind wings onto the thorax.*

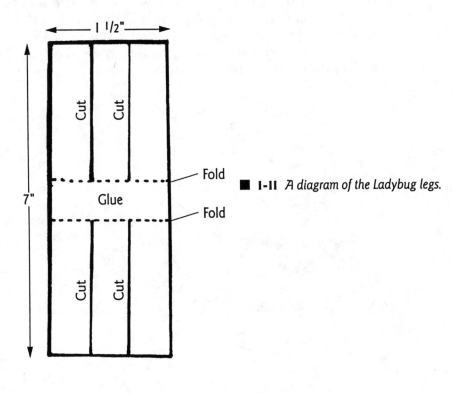

■ **1-11** *A diagram of the Ladybug legs.*

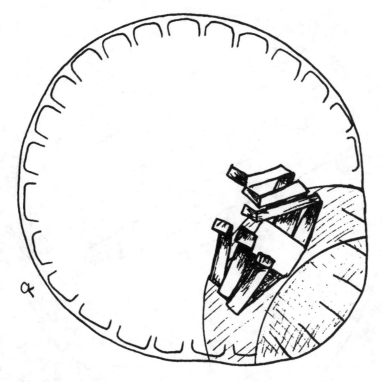

■ **1-12** *Glue the legs under the thorax.*

Let's Create Walnut Shell Ladybug Magnets

Learning about the anatomy of a beetle by creating a model; manipulating materials; learning about magnetic forces
To make your ladybug magnets (Fig. 1-13), purchase a bag of walnuts. Open each one by inserting a butter knife in the large end and pulling the knife down along the seam to force it into halves.

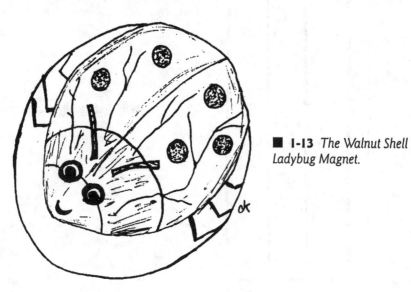

■ **1-13** *The Walnut Shell Ladybug Magnet.*

What you need

- ☐ Walnut shells opened into perfect halves (Large walnuts split into halves more easily than small ones.)
- ☐ Black permanent marker
- ☐ Paper punch
- ☐ Construction paper
- ☐ Poster paper
- ☐ Scissors
- ☐ White glue
- ☐ ½-inch-diameter or larger ceramic disc magnets (Buy them in a craft store. Do not use flexible strip magnets that can be cut with scissors. They do not work with this project.)
- ☐ Larger magnet or a magnetic wand (Available in a school supply store or catalog.)

Directions

1. Use a black permanent marker to draw a head on the wide end of the walnut shell. Draw a line to show the thorax. Draw a line to show the two hard outer front wings.
2. Use the pattern in Fig. 1-14 to trace a circle onto poster paper. Cut this out. Glue the ladybug in the middle of the circle. Draw six legs for the ladybug on the circle. Remember that a real beetle has six legs and that the legs are jointed. Draw legs that show these facts.

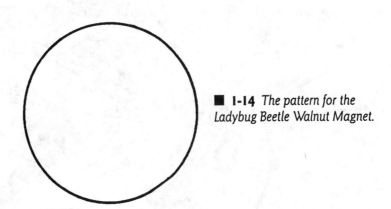

■ **1-14** *The pattern for the Ladybug Beetle Walnut Magnet.*

3. Glue on paper-punch eyes and paper-punch ladybug dots made of construction paper. Add two antennae made of skinny strips of paper ½ inch long.
4. Glue a magnet on the bottom of the circle. Set your ladybug on a Styrofoam tray or in the lid of a dress box or shoe box. Use a larger magnet or a magnetic wand to make your ladybug move.

Bee

☞ **Let's look at bees**

🔍 *Observing*
You can arrange to take a nature walk and look for bees; however, you might feel this activity is unsafe for the children. Other alternatives are to find a film or video of bees making honey or to have a beekeeper come speak to the children. Have informational books available to read. Let the children talk about times when they have seen bees and where they have seen bees (probably around flowers). Talk to the children about the caution they should take concerning bees.

A bee is the only insect that produces food eaten by people. There are about 10,000 kinds of bees, but honeybees are the kind that produce honey. We eat their honey and use the wax from their nests for making candles and lipsticks.

A honeybee (Fig. 1-15) starts out as a tiny, white egg. After several days, a tiny, worm-like larva comes out. The larva changes into a pupa and then emerges as an adult. This process takes about 20 days.

■ **1-15** *A Honeybee.*

A honeybee's body is divided into three sections: the head, the thorax, and the abdomen. The color of a honeybee can vary from black to light brown. Its body is covered with many little hairs. These hairs pick up pollen when the bee flies from flower to flower. Actually, the bee prefers to carry pollen with its feet.

A bee has five eyes. Three small eyes are on top of its head, and two compound eyes are on the sides of its head. A bee also has antennae on its head. The bee uses the antennae for smelling and feeling. A bee has a tongue to help it suck water and nectar. The tongue is on the outside of the head. It is tube-like and can bend all around. On the sides of the tongue, the bee has two jaws.

A bee has four wings on its thorax. The front wings are longer than the back wings. A bee can fly frontward, sideways, backward, and hover in place. A bee also has six legs on its thorax. Bees use their legs for walking, handling wax, and carrying pollen.

A bee has a stinger on its abdomen. The bee uses the stinger to defend itself. The stinger has hooks on the end of it. When the bee stings someone, the stinger is actually pulled out of the bee's body. Within a few hours after it stings someone, the bee dies.

Bees live and work together in groups. Like ants, a group of bees is called a colony. A bee might only live a few weeks or months, but the colony can go on functioning for years. A colony is made up of different kinds of honeybees: the queen, which lays the eggs; the workers, which gather food, make honey, and take care of the babies; and the drones, which are the male honeybees.

A hive is a nest where honey is stored. To build the hive, the workers make beeswax and shape it into a honeycomb. Special glands in the abdomen of the workers produce the wax. The honeycomb has many six-sided compartments called *cells*. The queen lays eggs in some of the cells. Pollen and nectar are stored in some of the cells. When worker bees suck up nectar from flowers, they store it in their honey stomachs. When they come back to the hive, they either give the nectar to the babies, or they store it in the cells. The worker bee adds certain chemicals to the nectar while it is in the bee's stomach. These chemicals allow the nectar to change to honey in the cells.

☞ *Let's taste honey*

🔍 *Observing*
Ask a parent or someone you know to give your class a jar of honey with some of the comb in it. Let the children use all of their five senses to examine the honey. Let the children orally complete the following:

This honey looks _____.

This honey smells _____.

When we pour the honey, I hear _____.

This honey feels _____.

This honey tastes _____.

Perhaps you might try a cooking activity with some recipes that use honey. Following this tasting experience, let the children write about it. If the children are too young to write by themselves, let them dictate sentences to you, and you can write them on a chart.

A worker bee goes out to collect pollen, nectar, and water for the baby bees. It flies all around, but when it is ready to go back to the nest, it takes a *beeline* back. A beeline means the shortest route.

☞ *Taking a beeline*

🔍 *Designing investigations; drawing conclusions; applying knowledge*

Take the children outside. You need to take a bell for you to ring. Tell the children to pretend they are bees looking for pollen, nectar, and water for their babies. They should fly all around until they hear your bell. When they hear the sound of the bell, they should run straight to you. Let four children do this activity at a time until everyone has had a chance. Ask them, "Why does a bee hurry home once it has found food and water for the baby bees?"

Sometimes a worker comes home and wants to tell the other bees about flowers it has found. It lets the others know by doing a dance. If the flowers are close by, the bee dances in a circle. If the flowers are far away, it dances in a figure eight. Then it dances in the direction of the flowers to let the others know where to go.

☞ *Dancing like bees*

🔍 *Science skill: Communicating information*

Let the children pretend to be bees and act out these dances. Use colored yarn or masking tape to make a circle and the number eight on the floor.

💡 *How do we communicate?*

🔍 *Communicating information*

"How do people show their excitement over something they have found? Let's pretend you and your friends love strawberries. You and your friends are outside playing. Your mother has just come home with a big basket of delicious strawberries. Think of different ways she can tell you about the strawberries and how to get to where they are." Let the children share and act out their ideas. Encourage them to think up a variety of ideas.

Let's Create a Cylinder Honeybee

🔍 *Learning about the anatomy of a honeybee by creating a model; manipulating materials including a cylinder; learning to measure and draw with a ruler; using reference material to find out about and create a honeybee*

An empty toilet paper cylinder makes a wonderful honeybee that flies on the end of a string (Fig. 1-16). This project can be used to teach measuring as each student measures and cuts out a rectangle with which to cover the cylinder. It can also be used to teach fractions; see step 2 on page 23.

What you need
☐ Toilet paper cylinder
☐ Ruler
☐ Pencil
☐ Scissors
☐ Yellow construction paper
☐ Construction paper in assorted colors

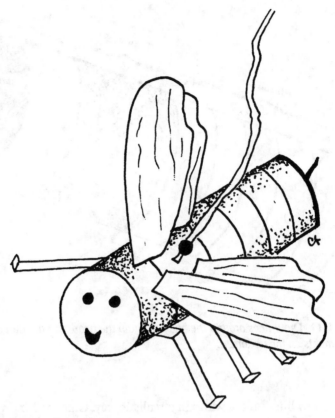

■ **1-16** *A Cylinder Honeybee.*

☐ Crayons
☐ White glue
☐ Paper fastener
☐ 24-inch piece of string
☐ Paper punch

Directions

1. Find a picture of a honeybee in a reference book.

2. Use the pencil and ruler to measure and draw a 4½-x-6-inch rectangle on yellow construction paper. Cut it out. [Another way to create the rectangle is to fold a piece of 9-x-12-inch yellow construction paper in half like a hot dog bun. Then fold it in half like a book. Cut on the fold lines to create four rectangles. Each rectangle is ¼ of the whole paper.]

3. Spread glue on the rectangle. Wrap it around the cylinder, covering the cylinder completely. The covered cylinder is the body of your honeybee.

4. Draw lines around the body to show which parts form the head, thorax, and abdomen (Fig. 1-17). Draw lines to show the segments of the abdomen. Color the thorax brown.

5. Use the patterns in Fig. 1-18 to trace two fore wings, two hind wings, and a circle-shaped head onto construction paper. Cut these shapes out.

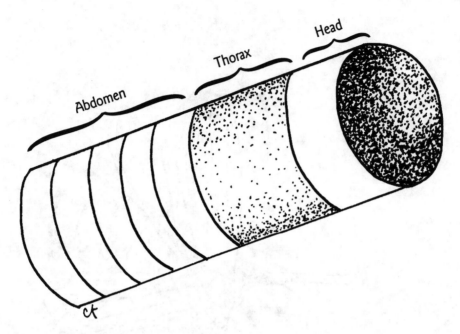

■ **1-17** *Draw lines around the body to show the head, thorax, and abdomen. Draw segments on the abdomen.*

6. Draw lines on the wings in a realistic way. Glue the hind wings to the top of the thorax, as shown in Fig. 1-16. Then glue on the fore wings. Each fore wing should slightly overlap each hind wing. Lay the honeybee flat with the wings down to dry for 30 minutes or longer.

7. To add the circle-shaped head, spread glue on the opening of the cylinder, and gently place the head over this opening.

8. Add eyes made from circles created by the paper punch. Make a stinger from paper. Glue it inside the tail of the bee.

9. An adult should make a small hole, using a scissor-tip, in the back of the bee. Insert a paper fastener through this hole. Use the ruler to measure a 24-inch piece of string or yarn. Tie it to the top of the fastener. Spread out the tabs of the fastener inside the cylinder to hold the string in place.

10. To create six legs, measure and cut out three ½-×-5½-inch construction paper rectangles. Put glue in the middle of each one. Stick the rectangles to the bottom thorax of the bee so they stick out straight at the sides. Bend each leg in half so that it hangs down.

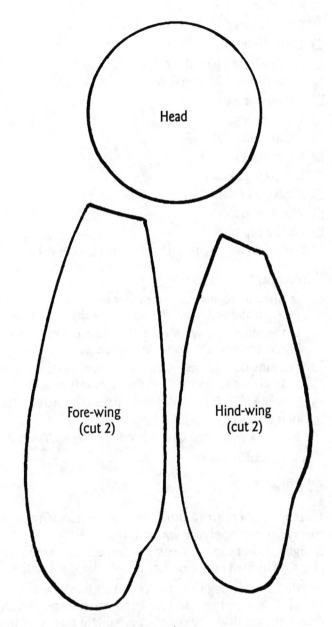

■ **I-18** *The patterns for the Cylinder Honeybee.*

Let's Create Honeybee Muffins

 Practicing kitchen chemistry; learning about dry measure and liquid measure; using whole numbers and fractions; learning to follow directions

Honey is the only sweetener used in these delicious muffins. They can be baked in the classroom in a toaster oven.

25

What you need
- [ ] 1 cup flour
- [ ] ½ cup whole wheat flour
- [ ] 2 teaspoons baking powder
- [ ] ¼ teaspoon salt
- [ ] 1 beaten egg
- [ ] ½ cup milk
- [ ] ½ cup honey
- [ ] ¼ cup cooking oil
- [ ] 2 mixing bowls
- [ ] Wooden spoon
- [ ] Muffin cup liners
- [ ] Muffin tin (A six-cup tin fits in most toaster ovens.)

Directions
1. In one mixing bowl, stir together the flour, whole wheat flour, baking powder, and salt. These items are the dry ingredients.
2. In the other mixing bowl, stir together the egg, milk, honey, and oil. These items are the liquid ingredients.
3. Pour the liquid ingredients all at once into the dry ingredients. Stir just until all of the dry ingredients are moistened. The batter will be lumpy.
4. Line the muffin tin with paper liners. Fill each muffin cup two-thirds full of batter.

5. Bake in a preheated 400°F oven for about 20 minutes or until golden.

Yield: 12 muffins

 ### Closure

Classifying; creating models; communicating and recording information; applying knowledge

Bringing closure to your study is important. Review your initial goals and give the children opportunities to talk about what they have learned.

As you move through the topics in this book, you can develop an ongoing mural. This mural should be a large visual display of all of the animals and their habitats. Begin by covering a bulletin board, or hanging on the wall, a large piece of blue bulletin board paper about 8 feet long. Let the children use construction paper to make a sun and white clouds for the sky. Let the children draw, color, or paint the insects you have studied or let them draw and color them on construction paper, cut them out, and glue them onto the mural. Have them add grass, dirt, and other parts of the animals' habitats.

You can add to the mural as the study goes on, so save room for other animals not yet covered in class. Plan ahead in your mind how you want the completed mural to look. Draw it out on paper and use the drawing as you move along in the study. The finished product will be magnificent, and everyone who sees it will learn from it.

Curriculum
Book

BUTTERFLIES

Science goals

To help children become aware of what butterflies are like, how they grow, what they do, and their purpose in the world

Teacher/Parent planning

Read through the first two activities. Borrow informational books from the library. Prepare to write words about butterflies on a large sheet of chart paper. Arrange for guest speakers and select videotapes to show to the class. An excellent video called *Butterflies* is available from Callaway Gardens, Ida Cason Callaway Foundation, Education Department, Pine Mountain, Georgia 31822, (404) 663-5153.

Materials needed for discussion and activities

☐ Informational books
☐ Chart paper
☐ Magnifying glasses
☐ Butterfly nursery
☐ Colored pipe cleaners from a craft store
☐ Construction paper
☐ Juice boxes with straws
☐ Butterfly garden (optional)

Related words

insect An animal that has six legs, a body that is divided into three parts, and a tough, shell-like covering

metamorphosis Changes in appearance, functions, and habits of an animal during its life

☞ *Getting ready for metamorphosis*

🔍 *Observing; manipulating materials; measuring; making predictions; recording information*

Look through school supply catalogs and purchase a butterfly nursery if you can. Several types are available that can be used over and over. One type is a box with transparent sides. Another type is made of a net fabric that allows visibility and air circulation. A certificate to order butterfly eggs comes with the nursery.

When you receive the eggs, they come in a special container with food for the caterpillars. If you cannot purchase a nursery, you can use a glass aquarium or any other container that allows space, visibility, and air circulation. You can still order the eggs from a catalog or you might be able to find eggs on host plants outdoors. You need the right type of food for the caterpillars, as well as twigs and leaves so that they can attach themselves to form the *chrysalis*.

After you get everything set up, create special journals for all the children so that they can record everything they observe. Let them record the dates of all changes, draw pictures, and keep other types of data about the events. Everyone will be entranced by watching the caterpillars come from the eggs, the caterpillars change to chrysalises, and the butterflies emerge. This whole process takes about three weeks. Several days after the butterflies emerge, you need to set them free outdoors. Plan a special ceremony for their release so that the children can feel a sense of reverence for these beautiful creatures. Videotape the ceremony if you can.

☞ *Getting ready for butterflies*

🔍 *Finding information; applying knowledge*

Before beginning your butterfly study, you might want to plant a small butterfly garden. To plant a garden, you need to find out which butterflies live in your area, what kinds of plants they need for laying their eggs on, what plants caterpillars like to eat, and from which flowers the butterflies like to sip nectar. Contact a local nature society for help. Recruit some parents to help with this project.

Choose a sunny location, preferably one that gets five to seven hours of sunlight each day. Be sure it is near a water source so you can give the garden plenty of water. Visit your local garden center to purchase plants. The following plants usually attract butterflies to sip nectar:

- ☐ Single marigolds
- ☐ Single zinnias
- ☐ Yellow cosmos
- ☐ Verbena
- ☐ Butterfly bush
- ☐ Lantana
- ☐ Dogwood trees
- ☐ Hawthorne trees
- ☐ Redbud trees
- ☐ Clover
- ☐ Rhododendrons
- ☐ Mint
- ☐ Thistle
- ☐ Black-eyed susans
- ☐ Honeysuckle
- ☐ Phlox
- ☐ Sunflowers
- ☐ Milkweed
- ☐ Zinnias
- ☐ Purple Coneflowers
- ☐ Yarrows
- ☐ Asters
- ☐ Chives
- ☐ Shasta Daisies
- ☐ Liatris

☐ Lavenders
☐ Coreopsis

The following plants are examples that are called *host plants*. Butterflies lay their eggs on these plants, the caterpillars feed on them after the eggs hatch. Black swallowtail caterpillars eat parsley and dill. Monarch butterfly caterpillars eat milkweeds. If the correct host plant is not available, the caterpillar starves to death. The following list contains examples of host plants:

☐ Parsley
☐ Dill
☐ Butterfly weed
☐ Nasturtium
☐ Milkweeds
☐ Clover
☐ Alfalfa
☐ Violets
☐ Plantain
☐ Snapdragon
☐ Verbena
☐ Thistle
☐ Sunflower
☐ Aspen trees
☐ Cherry trees
☐ Poplar trees
☐ Willow trees

Butterflies lay their eggs on a suitable host plant. After your host plants start to grow, you will find butterfly eggs in your garden. Then you can clip the stem (with the eggs on it) off the host plant and put it in a butterfly nursery. The chrysalis stage might take place in your butterfly garden or the caterpillars might crawl out to a tree or shrub.

A proper butterfly garden (Fig. 2-1) should have the following elements:

1. *Direct sunlight* Butterflies are cold-blooded and need warmth to fly. The plants also need direct sunlight to grow well.
2. *Water* Butterflies need water. Out in nature, butterflies sip water from puddles. Use a shallow container of water so that the butterflies do not drown. A dish with pebbles in it works well.
3. *Rocks* Butterflies need stones to sit on so they can bask in the sun.
4. *Wildflowers* Butterflies are attracted to particular colors. Their favorite colors are purple, yellow, orange and red.
5. *Protection from wind* Butterflies like still air. Plant some tall plants to provide protection from the wind.
6. *Protection from pesticides* Butterflies are sensitive to pesticides. Never use any kind of insect repellent around your garden. It kills butterflies.

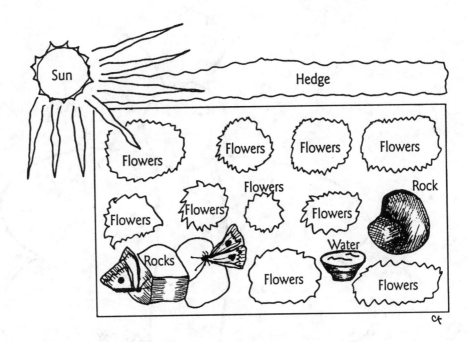

■ **2-1** *A Butterfly Garden.*

☞ *Butterfly pretest*

🔍 *Communicating information*

Give each child a blank piece of paper and a crayon or pencil. Tell the children to draw a butterfly on the paper. Put names and dates on the papers and collect them. Look at the drawings and analyze what you see. You might find that the children drew a butterfly that looks like the drawing in Fig. 2-2.

Most children's drawings have two body parts instead of three. Instead of four wings, the children probably drew two wings. Now you can see some of the misconceptions you need to correct. Save these drawings and do a posttest at the end of the study.

☞ *Let's find butterflies*

🔍 *Observing*

Plan to undertake this study in the spring, summer, or fall when butterflies are easily available to observe. Take a walk with your children. Look for butterflies. Remind the children to walk quietly and never bother any butterfly that you see. Encourage them to watch and listen. After you get back to the classroom, talk about the butterflies you observed, what they looked like, how they moved, where they were, and how quiet and graceful these insects are.

A butterfly is a colorful insect known for its beauty and graceful way of flying. Butterflies are found all over the world. Butterflies lived on earth even before dinosaurs. Some butterflies live only a few weeks and some live about a year. Butterflies need food, water, and shelter. (You should share the information about a butterfly garden that precedes this section.)

■ **2-2** *A child's drawing for the butterfly pretest.*

All butterflies go through four stages in their lifetime. This process of changes is called *metamorphosis*. First, the butterfly is an egg. Its mother lays the egg on a plant that can give the offspring food after it hatches. Butterfly eggs can be green, yellow, orange, or red.

Inside the egg, a caterpillar begins to grow. After a few days or even months, when it gets just the right size, it comes out of the egg. A caterpillar has a head and a body that is made up of 12 parts called *segments*. Caterpillars are smooth or fuzzy, might have two little horns on its head, and can be brightly striped or plain. The caterpillar is so hungry when it first comes out that it eats the eggshell, which contains nutrients for its growth. Then it begins to eat certain leaves or other kinds of foods. It grows and grows. The caterpillar's skin does not grow, so it splits open and comes off three or four times.

☞ *Where are the caterpillars?*

 Drawing conclusions

You can have fun with the children doing this activity. Get some colorful, fuzzy pipe cleaners from a craft store. Cut them into pieces about 2 inches long. These pieces can be "caterpillars." While the children are out of the room, place the caterpillars all around the room. Try to place each one on something of the same color so that the caterpillars are camouflaged and hard to find. Be sure you have enough caterpillars for everyone. When the children return, tell them this story:

"Children, while you were gone, a whole bunch of caterpillars came into the room. I had to leave for a minute and when I came back, I couldn't find them. I want you to help me find them. Let's walk quietly around the room with only whisper voices and look for the caterpillars. When you see one, pick it up and take it to your seat. It can be your friend for the day."

When everyone has found a caterpillar, ask the children why they think the caterpillars hid where they did. Guide them as they discover that animals try to hide themselves for safety.

Let's Create Caterpillar Magnets

Learning about the anatomy of a caterpillar by creating a model; manipulating materials; learning about magnetic forces

A 12-inch pipe cleaner from a craft store makes a wiggly caterpillar when a magnet controls its movement (Fig. 2-3).

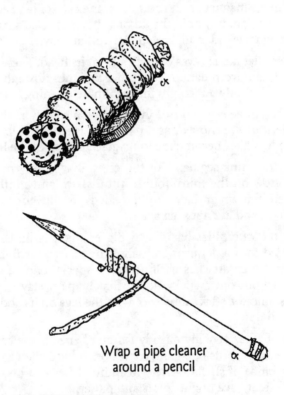

Wrap a pipe cleaner
around a pencil

■ **2-3** *How to make the Caterpillar Magnet.*

What you need
☐ 12-inch pipe cleaner
☐ Pencil
☐ Paper punch

☐ Black marker
☐ Construction paper
☐ White glue
☐ Ceramic disc magnets, ½-inch diameter or larger (Buy these in a craft store.)
☐ Second larger magnet or a magnetic wand (Buy this in a school supply store or order from a catalog.)
☐ Shoe box or Styrofoam tray

Directions

1. Wrap the pipe cleaner around a pencil to coil it.
2. Use a paper punch to create two eyes from construction paper. A caterpillar actually has twelve eyes! To create these, use a marker to draw six dots on each paper punch circle. Glue the paper-punch eyes on the end of the caterpillar.
3. Glue a magnet on the bottom of the caterpillar. Set your caterpillar on a Styrofoam tray or in the lid of a shoe box. Use a larger magnet or a magnet wand to make your caterpillar move.

A caterpillar has six eyes on each side of its head. These eyes help the caterpillar tell light from dark. A caterpillar breathes through small holes along the sides of its body. Air comes through these openings to all parts of its body.

The first three segments of the caterpillar's body make up the thorax. Each segment of the thorax has a pair of jointed legs with tiny claws at the tip. These legs later become the long, graceful legs of the butterfly.

The other nine segments of the caterpillar's body make up the abdomen. Legs grow on the third, fourth, fifth, sixth, and ninth segments of the abdomen, but when the caterpillar sheds its skin for the last time, these legs come off and are not seen again.

After the caterpillar has grown big enough, it finds a special place to be changed into a *pupa*, or chrysalis. The caterpillar finds a twig or a leaf, to which it then attaches itself. It uses a special part of its head, called a *spinneret*, to put out a sticky liquid that helps it stay in place. The caterpillar holds onto the sticky substance with the legs on its abdomen and hangs with its head down.

The pupa has actually already formed beneath the caterpillar's skin. When the last skin splits open and comes off, a hard shell forms around the pupa. Some kinds of shells are very beautiful. They can be silver or gold in color. They might have bright colors and patterns.

Caterpillar Corner *The word* chrysalis *comes from a greek word meaning gold.*

The chrysalis does not eat. It stays in its special place for 10 days or many months, depending on the kind of butterfly it will become. Inside the chrysalis, a marvelous change takes place.

At the right time, the butterfly comes out of this final shell covering. At first, the butterfly's wings are damp and crumpled up. Eventually, the butterfly pumps air throughout its body and wings. Its exoskeleton hardens and the wings flatten and spread out. Within a couple of hours, the butterfly is ready to fly.

Let's Create a Butterfly Life-Cycle Wheel

Learning about the life cycle of a butterfly by creating a model; manipulating materials; learning to draw with a ruler; using reference material to find out about a butterfly

Draw pictures showing the four stages of the butterfly's life cycle. Then create a window that turns, so each stage can be seen separately (Fig. 2-4).

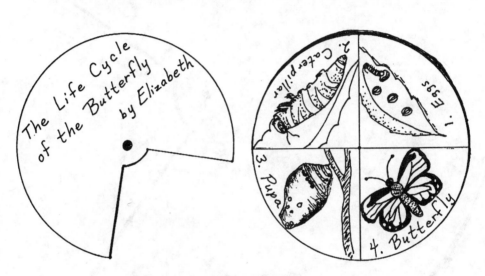

■ **2-4** *How to make the Butterfly Life Cycle Wheel.*

What you need

☐ Construction paper
☐ Scissors
☐ Ruler
☐ Markers or crayons
☐ Paper fastener

Directions

1. Use the patterns in Figs. 2-5 and 2-6 to draw the top and bottom life-cycle wheels. Cut them out.
2. Using a ruler, draw straight lines on the bottom wheel to create four sections, as shown on the pattern. Number each section.
3. Draw caterpillar eggs in section number one. Draw a caterpillar in section number two. Draw a pupa (chrysalis) in section number three. Draw a butterfly in section number four. Label each section.

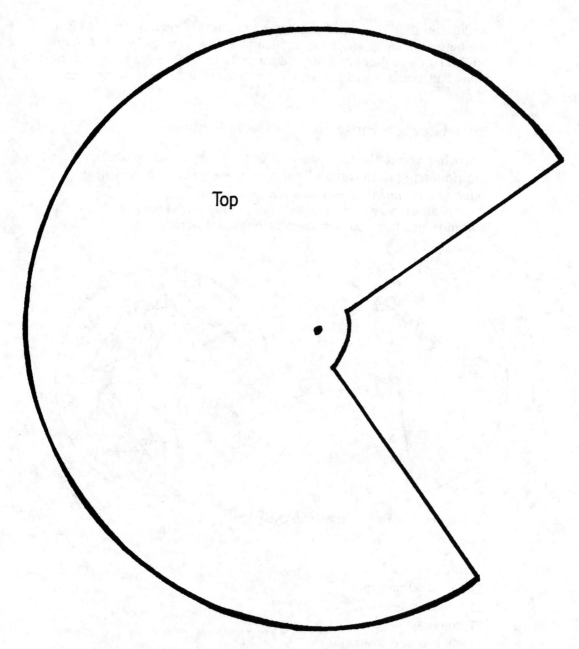

Top

■ **2-5** *The pattern for the Butterfly Life Cycle Wheel.*

4. Fasten the top life-cycle wheel onto the bottom one by inserting a paper fastener through the center of both. Label the top wheel by writing "The Life Cycle of the Butterfly."

The butterfly has three body parts: the head, thorax, and abdomen. The butterfly has two large eyes, which are made up of thousands of little eyes. A butterfly is sensitive to movement and color. Between its eyes are two *antennae*. Each antenna has a thick tip called a *club*. A butterfly uses its antennae to smell flowers and other food.

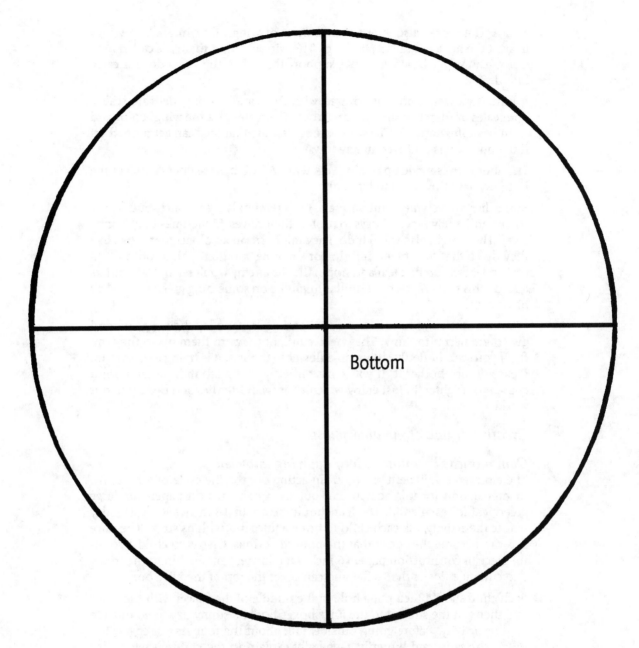

Bottom

■ **2-6** *The pattern for the Butterfly Life Cycle Wheel.*

A butterfly can't bite or chew. It can only have liquids as food. It has a *proboscis*, which is a long, thin tube that can sip up liquids. The proboscis works like a straw that goes deep into flowers to sip nectar and water. The butterfly might also drink the juice of very ripe fruit. When the butterfly doesn't need to drink anything, it curls up the proboscis beneath its head.

The middle part of a butterfly, the thorax, supports six legs, three on each side. Each leg has a foot and claws that help the butterfly walk and cling to things. Many butterflies have very short front legs that you might not even notice. The thorax also supports two pairs of wings, four in all. The wings nearest the head are called *fore wings*. The wings behind them are called *hind wings*. The wings have veins that support them, but the veins do not carry blood.

A butterfly's whole body is covered with thousands of tiny, delicate scales. The scales overlap like shingles on a roof. The scales give the wings color and form beautiful patterns. The scales are so delicate that they can get rubbed off if the butterfly is bothered in any way.

The abdomen is made up of nine segments. All of these segments, except the last one, have tiny holes to let in air.

Butterflies are very peaceful animals. Other animals try to catch butterflies, so butterflies have special ways to protect themselves. Sometimes they just fly away. They might also try to hide. They might sit on an object that looks like they do so that they blend into it. For example, a butterfly that looks like a certain leaf sits on that leaf and hopes that its enemy won't see it. Caterpillars also do this trick. A green caterpillar might lie on something green so it won't be noticed.

What do butterflies need? They need special plants to lay their eggs on and give them nectar to drink. They need sunlight to warm them up so they can fly. If you see a butterfly sitting on a flower in the sun, it is trying to get warm. Please do not bother it. If you see a butterfly flying around, please do not chase it or frighten it. Just enjoy watching it fly. Butterflies add beauty to our world.

 Creative drama of metamorphosis

Communicating information; applying knowledge

The children can benefit greatly from acting out the life cycle of a butterfly. In preparation for this activity, cut out from construction paper one large green leaf for each child. The leaf should be about 18 inches long. The day before the activity, ask each child to bring a juice box with its straw. The juice box can become the nectar that the butterfly drinks. Give each child a colorful piece of construction paper (6 inches × 6 inches) and let him or her draw and cut out a flower that is flat and can cover the top of the juice box.

Each child should then put a hole in the middle of the flower with the straw and then put the straw into the juice box. Choose a sunny day to go outside for this activity. Before going outside, talk about the four stages: egg, caterpillar, chrysalis, and butterfly. Generally explain to the children what they will be doing outside. Once you are outside, let each child lay his or her juice box flower down on the ground in its own special place where he or she can find it later.

Now lay a construction paper leaf down on the ground and direct a child to curl up on it like an egg. Continue until all the "eggs" are on leaves. Next, tell the children that they are hatching out of their eggs as caterpillars. They should eat their eggshell and then pretend to eat their leaf. Next, they need to find a place to shed their skin and form a chrysalis. (Let them think of creative ways to do this step.) Finally, tell them to slowly come out of the chrysalis, slowly stretch out their wings, and eventually fly around. Encourage the children to fly gracefully. At any time, they can stop at their special flower and sip "nectar," then continue flying.

☞ *Types of butterflies*

🔍 *Applying knowledge*

Have the children look through reference books for information on butterflies. Talk with them about what they find. Tell them that they are going to learn about several kinds of butterflies.

Spring Azure

Many kinds of butterflies are blue. One kind is called the *spring azure*. It can be found throughout the United States. When it is a caterpillar, it lives on dogwood, sumac, lilac, and other types of flowering trees and shrubs. The caterpillar is only about ½ inch long. It has a brown head and a pale body. It has one dark stripe down its back and some green stripes on each side. When it becomes a butterfly, it is very small and is blue. It visits plum and peach blossoms to sip nectar.

Let's Create a Little Book:
The Adventures of a Spring Azure Butterfly

🔍 *Using reference material to find out about a spring azure butterfly; learning about the anatomy of a butterfly by drawing a lifelike picture; recording information by drawing and writing*

The spring azure butterfly is very small and brightly colored. Create a lifelike model that "flies" on a narrow ribbon from adventure to adventure inside of a little book (Fig 2-7).

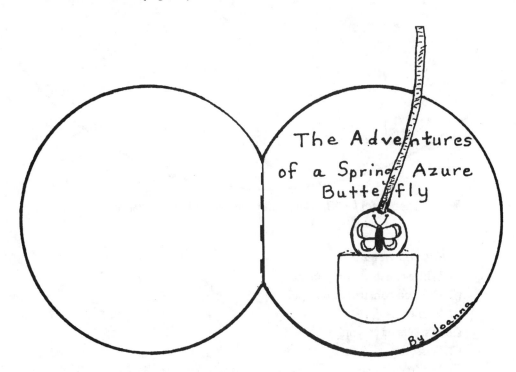

■ **2-7** *Let's create a Little Book.*

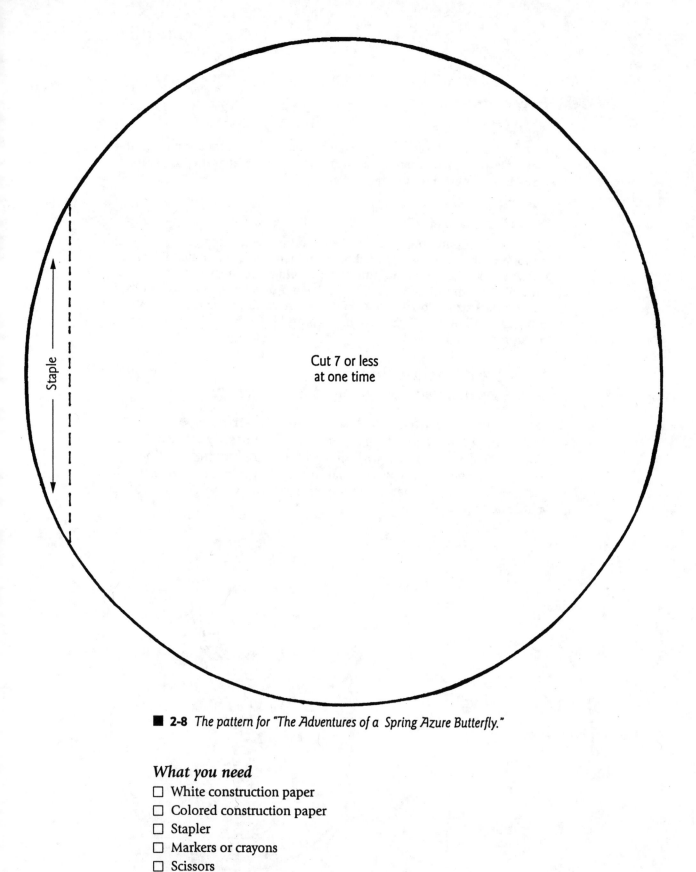

Staple

Cut 7 or less
at one time

■ **2-8** *The pattern for "The Adventures of a Spring Azure Butterfly."*

What you need
☐ White construction paper
☐ Colored construction paper
☐ Stapler
☐ Markers or crayons
☐ Scissors
☐ White glue
☐ 18-inch-long × ¼-inch-wide ribbon (45 mm × 6 mm)

Directions

1. Use the pattern in Fig. 2-8 to draw seven (or fewer) large circles on white construction paper. An easy way to do this step is to stack seven pages of paper, draw the circle on the top page, staple the seven circles together as shown on the pattern, and then cut through all seven pages at the same time.

2. Create a large flower picture for the cover of your book by ripping and tearing flower petals out of colored construction paper and gluing them onto the cover.

3. Use the pattern in Fig. 2-9 to trace and cut out a pocket and a spring azure butterfly. Glue the pocket inside the front of the book. Color the butterfly. (Remember that a spring azure butterfly is blue!) Attach a narrow ribbon 18 inches (45 mm) long to the butterfly by cutting a slit in the butterfly circle, inserting the ribbon, and gluing the end of the ribbon onto itself.

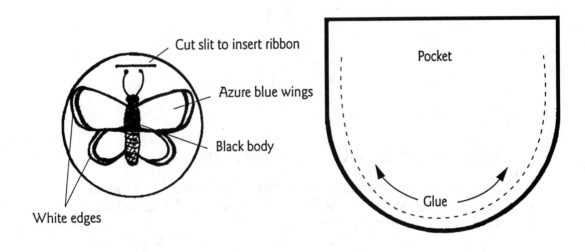

■ **2-9** *The patterns for the pocket and the Spring Azure Butterfly.*

4. Fill the book with the adventures of your spring azure butterfly through stories and drawings. When your book is finished, fly your butterfly from page to page on the end of its ribbon. Store it in the pocket.

Swallowtail

Swallowtail butterflies have special wings that no other butterflies have. On each hind wing is a slender, pointed tip or tail. Swallowtails borrow their name from a kind of bird called a swallow because these wingtips resemble the long, pointed wings of that bird.

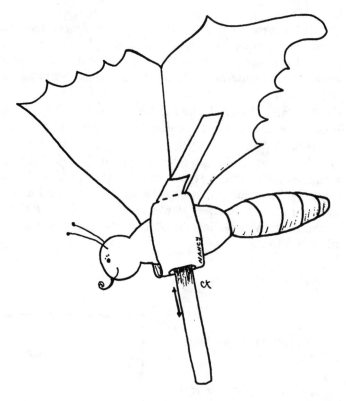

■ **2-10** *The Swallowtail Butterfly.*

Let's Create a Yellow Swallowtail Butterfly

Learning about the anatomy of a butterfly by creating a model; manipulating materials; learning to measure and draw with a ruler; using reference material

The Yellow Swallowtail butterfly model is created from four pattern pieces. The finished butterfly softly flaps its wings when you move the midsection up and down (Fig. 2-10).

What you need

☐ 12-×-18-inch yellow construction paper
☐ Half a file folder or similar light-weight cardboard
☐ Two pieces of 1-×-10-inch cardboard (Cut from a cardboard box.)
☐ Scissors
☐ Crayons
☐ Markers
☐ White glue
☐ Curling ribbon
☐ Paper punch

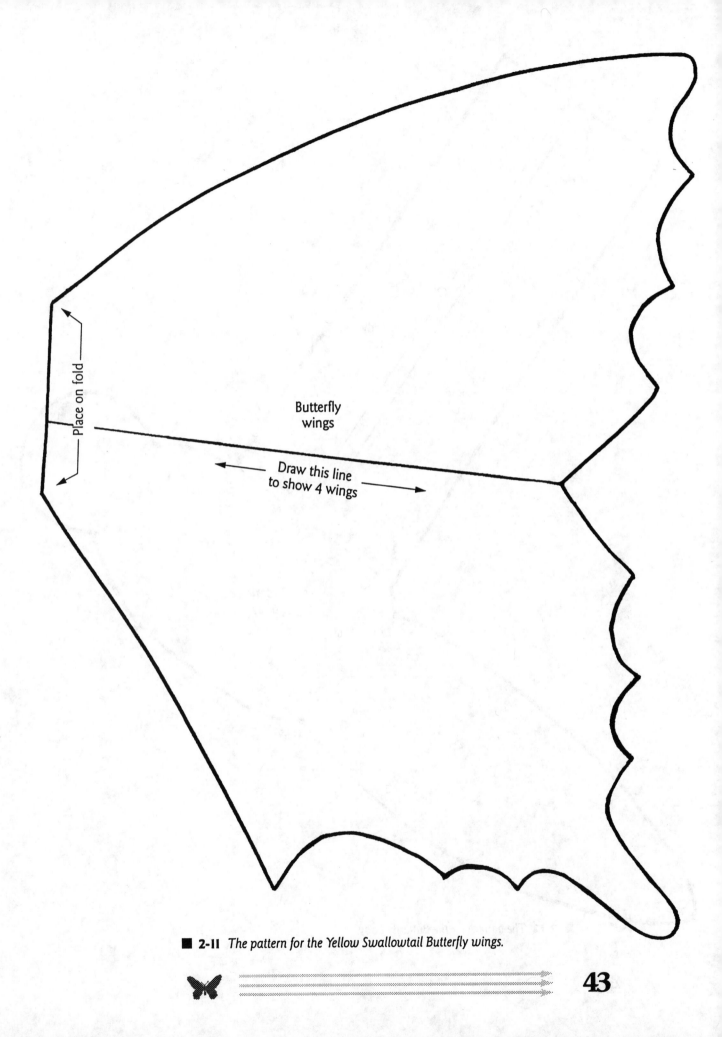

Place on fold

Butterfly wings

Draw this line to show 4 wings

■ **2-11** *The pattern for the Yellow Swallowtail Butterfly wings.*

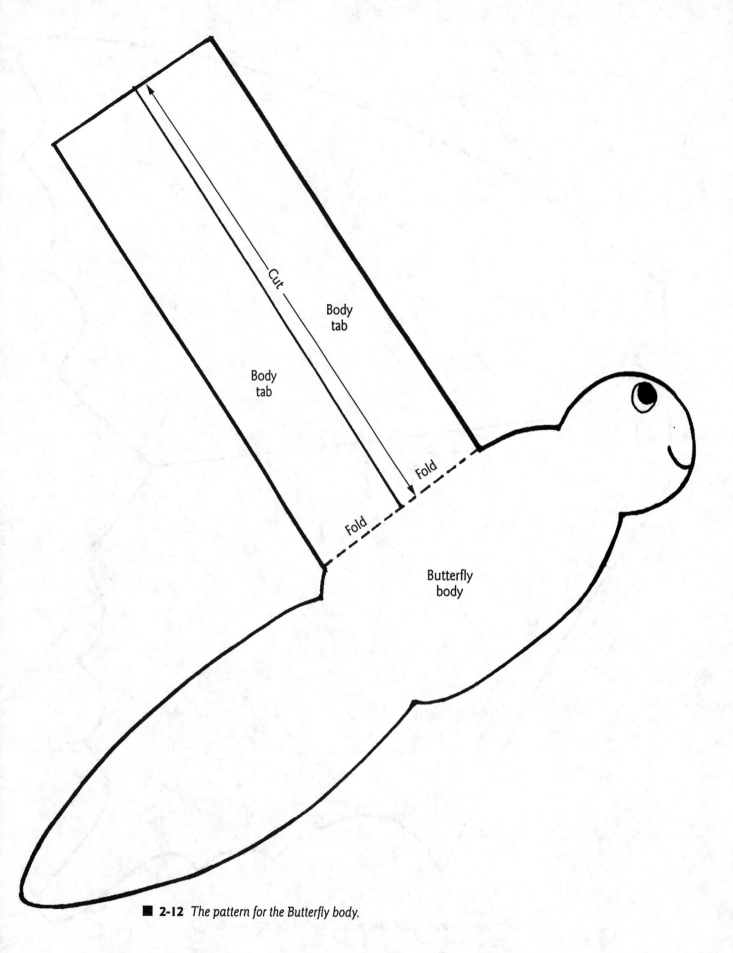

■ **2-12** *The pattern for the Butterfly body.*

Directions

1. Find a picture of a yellow swallowtail butterfly in a reference book in your library or media center.

2. To create a realistic model, fold a sheet of yellow construction paper in half like a book. Use the pattern in Fig. 2-11 on page 43 to trace the wings onto this paper. Cut out the wings. Open them. Color the wings on both sides to look like a real butterfly. Because the wings must be made from a single piece of paper, you need to draw a heavy line across them to show where the fore wings and the hind wings overlap.

3. Use the two patterns in Figs. 2-12 on page 44 and 2-13 to trace the body and the midsection onto half a file folder. Color them on both sides with crayons, and cut them out. Use a marker to draw eyes on the head. Draw segments on the abdomen.

4. Put glue on the body tabs and glue the body underneath the middle of the wings (Fig. 2-14).

5. Glue one stick on each side of the body, and then glue the sticks together to make a single strong handle for the butterfly (Fig. 2-15).

6. Cut a slit in the midsection as shown on the pattern. Insert the stick in this slit. Slide the midsection up the stick until it touches the body. Glue the tabs of the midsection (shown on the pattern) to the underside of the wings (Fig. 2-10). The midsection will look like a little tent over the body of the butterfly. Lay your butterfly upside down and let the glue dry for an hour.

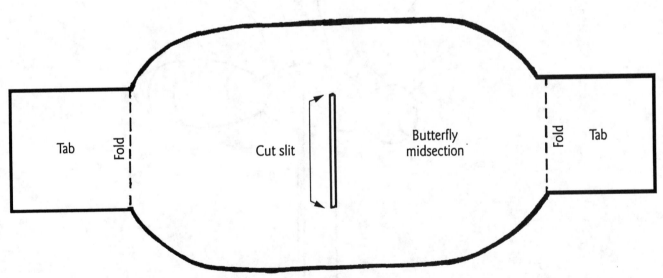

■ **2-13** *The pattern for the Butterfly midsection.*

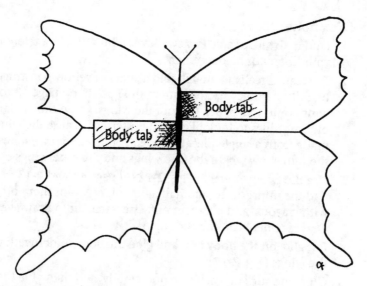

■ **2-14** *Glue the body under the wings.*

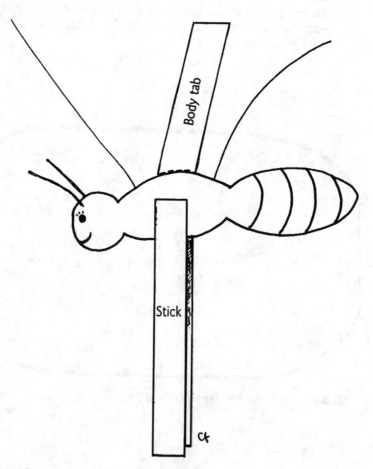

■ **2-15** *Glue one stick to each side of the body.*

7. Glue on a proboscis made of curling ribbon. Add skinny antennae cut from file folder scraps. Glue a club made from a paper punch on the end of each antenna.

8. To make the wings flap, hold the stick in one hand and move the midsection up and down with the other hand.

A Painted Lady Butterfly

Painted lady butterflies can be found throughout the world. They can fly long distances. The painted lady butterfly has shades of brown, black, and yellow on its wings. (The eggs of this butterfly are the kind you usually receive with a butterfly nursery.)

Let's Create a Painted Lady Butterfly Cylinder

Learning about the anatomy of a butterfly by creating a model; manipulating materials including a cylinder; learning to measure and draw with a ruler; using reference material to find out about and create a painted lady butterfly

A toilet paper roll cylinder can be used to create a painted lady butterfly that softly flaps its wings on the end of a ribbon or yarn (Fig. 2-16). This project can be used to teach measuring as each student measures and cuts out a rectangle with which to cover the cylinder. It can also be used to teach fractions; see step 2 in the following directions.

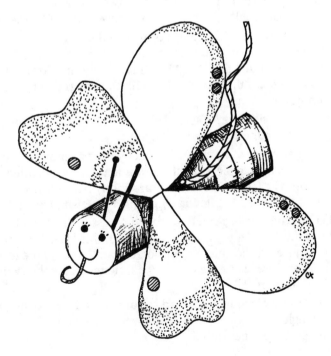

■ **2-16** *A Cylinder Painted Lady Butterfly.*

What you need

- ☐ Toilet paper cylinder
- ☐ Ruler
- ☐ Pencil
- ☐ Scissors
- ☐ Yellow construction paper
- ☐ White construction paper
- ☐ Crayons
- ☐ White glue
- ☐ Paper fastener
- ☐ 24-inch piece of yarn or narrow ribbon
- ☐ Paper punch

Directions

1. Find a picture of a painted lady butterfly in a reference book.

2. Use the pencil and ruler to measure and draw a 4½-x-6-inch rectangle on yellow construction paper. Cut it out. [Another way to create the rectangle is to fold a piece of 9-x-12-inch yellow construction paper in half like a hot dog bun. Then fold it in half like a book. Cut on the fold lines to create four rectangles. Each rectangle is ¼ of the whole paper.]

3. Spread glue on the rectangle. Wrap it around the cylinder, covering the cylinder completely. The covered cylinder is the body of your butterfly.

4. Draw lines around the body to show which parts form the head, thorax, and abdomen (Fig. 2-16). Draw lines to show the segments of the abdomen. Color the thorax brown.

5. Use the patterns in Fig. 2-17 to trace two fore wings, two hind wings, and a circle head onto white construction paper. Cut these parts out.

6. Color the wings with orange, brown, and black crayons in a realistic way. Glue the hind wings to the top of the thorax, as shown in Fig. 2-18. Then glue on the fore wings. Each fore wing should slightly overlap each hind wing. Lay the butterfly flat with the wings down to dry for 30 minutes or longer.

7. To add the circle head, spread glue on the opening of the cylinder, and gently place the head on this opening.

8. Add eyes made from circles created by the paper punch. Make a proboscis from a piece of gift ribbon that has been curled with the scissors. Create two antennae from skinny paper strips 2 inches long. Add a club to each antenna by gluing a paper-punch circle to the end.

9. Let an adult make a small hole with a scissor-tip in the back of the butterfly. Insert a paper fastener through this hole. Use the ruler to measure a 24-inch piece of ribbon or yarn. Tie it to the top of the fastener. Spread out the tabs of the fastener inside the cylinder to hold the ribbon in place.

10. To create six legs, measure and cut out a 1-x-3-inch construction paper rectangle. Make two 1-inch cuts in each end. Bend the legs up or down, and glue them beneath the thorax.

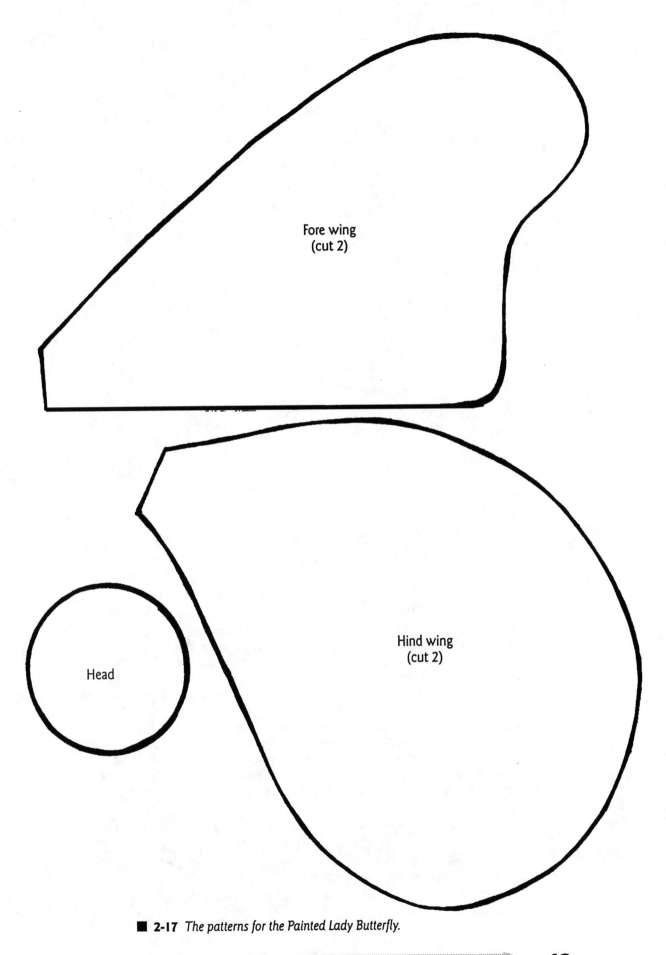

2-17 *The patterns for the Painted Lady Butterfly.*

Fore wing
(cut 2)

Hind wing
(cut 2)

Head

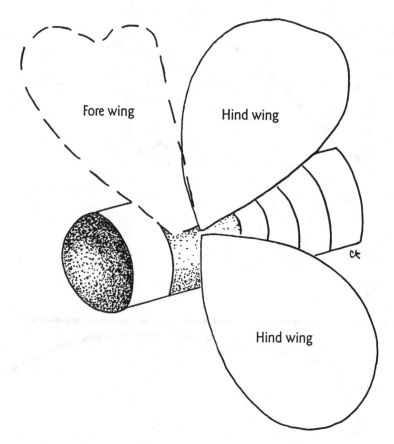

■ **2-18** *Glue the hind wings to the top of the thorax. Add the fore wings.*

Monarch Butterfly

A monarch butterfly is orange and black. Monarch butterflies lay their eggs on milkweed plants. When the caterpillars come out, they eat the milkweed leaves. They change to the chrysalis stage and soon emerge as butterflies. The ones born in the spring and early summer live about a month, but the ones born at the end of summer can live for many months. Before winter comes, they go on a long flight and thousands of monarch butterflies might fly together. Some of them come from Canada and from the Rocky Mountains. Some fly to California and some fly all the way to Mexico because they need a warm place to spend the winter. They need flowers to sip nectar from, such as foxglove, buttercups, and marigolds. During February, the mother monarchs lay eggs on milkweed plants. The monarchs that are born start to fly back northward.

Caterpillar Corner *The migration back north is quite complex and you might not want to share this part, but it is very interesting. The first spring generation from Mexico reaches the southern states in April or May. The second generation of butterflies reaches Virginia and Delaware by June. By early summer, the third generation reaches the Great Lakes and the southern part of Canada.*

Let's Create a Butterfly Sand Painting

Learning about the anatomy of a butterfly by creating a picture; manipulating materials; using reference material
Create a beautiful, unusual butterfly picture with colored "sand" made of dry cereal and food dye (Fig. 2-19).

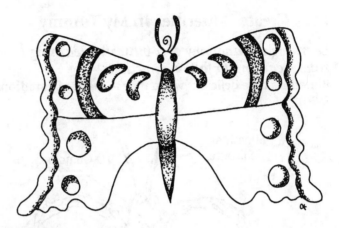

■ **2-19** *A Butterfly Sand Painting.*

What you need
☐ 12-×18-inch white construction paper
☐ Pencil
☐ Dry grits, Cream of Wheat, or Cream of Rice
☐ Red, green, blue, and yellow liquid food dyes
☐ Plastic sandwich bags with twist ties
☐ Wax paper
☐ Milk lid
☐ White glue
☐ Watercolor brush

Directions
1. Find color pictures of butterflies in your media center or library. Use a pencil to draw the outline of a butterfly on a large sheet of white construction paper. Make your drawing big enough to fill the whole page. Be sure to include the following:
   • A head with two clubbed antennae
   • A thorax with four wings attached
   • An abdomen
2. Pour 1 tablespoon of dry cereal into a plastic sandwich bag. Add three drops of food dye. Close the bag with a twist tie. Shake the bag until the cereal is dyed. Do the same thing with three more sandwich bags, adding a different dye color to each bag.
3. Put wax paper under your drawing. Squirt glue into a milk lid. Dip the brush into the glue, then paint the glue onto a part of your butterfly

drawing. Sprinkle one color of cereal onto the wet glue. Shake off the extra cereal onto the wax paper and return it to its bag. Continue painting parts of your drawing with glue, adding different colors each time.

4. When your butterfly painting is finished, lay it flat to dry. Wash out your brush with soap and water.

Let's Create Butterflies in My Tummy

Learning the anatomy of a butterfly; learning to measure with a ruler; learning to follow directions
Butterflies taste delicious when they're made of gumdrops and pretzels (Fig. 2-20)!

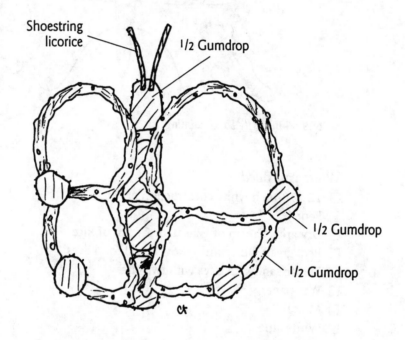

Shoestring licorice

¹/2 Gumdrop

¹/2 Gumdrop

¹/2 Gumdrop

Gumdrops

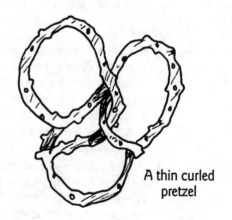

A thin curled pretzel

■ **2-20** *Butterflies in My Tummy.*

What you need

- ☐ Gumdrops
- ☐ Thin, curled pretzels
- ☐ Shoestring licorice
- ☐ Paper plate
- ☐ Children's scissors
- ☐ Ruler
- ☐ Drawing paper
- ☐ Crayons

Directions

1. Cut two gumdrops in half with clean scissors and line them up on the plate, sticky side up. The top gumdrop is the head of the butterfly. The second gumdrop is the thorax. The third and fourth gumdrops are the abdomen.
2. Nibble a curled pretzel until a piece with two connected sections remains. Stick this onto the thorax (the second gumdrop) to form two wings. Repeat nibbling and sticking with another pretzel to make two more wings.
3. Nibble a shoestring licorice candy to make two 1-inch antennae. Use the ruler to measure them. Stick them to the head of the butterfly.
4. Cut two more gumdrops into circles, and stick them on the pretzel wings as decorations.
5. Before eating your creation, draw a picture of it with crayons. Be sure to include the three body parts of your insect, the two antennae, and the four wings. Entitle your drawing "Butterflies in My Tummy."

☞ Butterfly post-test

Applying knowledge

Give the children a blank piece of white paper and ask them to draw a butterfly. If this unit of study has been effective, you should see dramatic differences in the drawings as you compare these tests with the pretest. Hopefully, you will see three body parts and four wings. Date the papers and staple the two papers together.

☞ Closure

Classifying; creating models; communicating and recording information; applying knowledge

Bringing closure to your study is important. Review your initial goals and give the children opportunities to talk about what they have learned.

1. Continue adding to the ongoing mural as described in the closure section of Chapter 1. Help the children create a butterfly garden with beautiful butterflies all around.

2. Let the children write songs using familiar tunes. For example, you could use the tune to "Mary Had a Little Lamb" and write something like the following:

(A child's name) saw a little butterfly,
A little butterfly, a little butterfly,
(A child's name) saw a little butterfly,
Its wings were as blue as the sky.

You might write a song to the tune of "Did You Ever See A Lassie?"

Did you ever see a butterfly, a butterfly, a butterfly,
Did you ever see a butterfly
Flying around?
Flying this way and that way,
Flying this way and that way.
Did you ever see a butterfly flying around?

MOTHS

Science goals

To help children become aware of what moths are like, how they grow, what they do, and their purpose in the world

Teacher/Parent planning

See the first activity "Find A Cocoon." Borrow informational books from the library or the media center at your school. Get magnifying glasses. Prepare to write words about moths on a large sheet of chart paper.

Materials needed for discussion and activities

☐ Informational books
☐ Chart paper
☐ Magnifying glasses
☐ Cocoon
☐ Container to keep cocoon

Related words

insect An animal that has six legs, a body that is divided into three different parts, and has a tough, shell-like covering

metamorphosis Changes in the appearance, functions, and habits of an animal during its life

☞ *Find a cocoon*

 Observing; designing investigations

Send a note home to parents to enlist their help in finding a cocoon. Cocoons can be found on screened porches, decks, tree twigs, or even on the ground in the woods.

You can put it in a container like the butterfly nursery, so that the children can watch and feel. You should just lay it in the nursery. The children can gently touch it or hold it. Have magnifying glasses available. Occasionally, dampen the cocoon with water. Be prepared to set the moth free within a day after it comes out. It might be weeks or months before this happens.

Moths are relatives of butterflies. They are like butterflies in many ways, but different in some ways too. Generally, butterflies fly during the daytime and moths fly at night; however, some moths fly during the day. Since many moths are out at night, we miss seeing them. The best place to find moths is near a light outdoors. Moths are attracted to fluorescent lights. Most moths are not as colorful as butterflies. Many moths are brownish in color. The antennae of moths look like feathery rabbit ears or are smooth and tapered, while the antennae of butterflies are more slender and have little clubs on the ends. When a moth is resting, it holds its wings out flat over its body; a butterfly holds it wings up over its back.

A moth begins its life as an egg, which is laid on a plant or other things like fabric from which our clothes are made (especially wool and silk). When the caterpillar hatches, it begins to eat the plant or whatever material on which it is living. As the caterpillar grows, it sheds its skin and grows some more. Shedding the skin can happen as much as ten times.

A moth caterpillar has 1 mouth, 12 eyes and 2 antennae. It chews its food. A spinneret sticks out below its mouth. Liquid silk comes out of the spinneret. The silk hardens and helps the caterpillar stay in one place.

The body is divided into 12 parts. The first three parts after the head make up the thorax. Each part of the thorax has a pair of legs. These legs become the legs of the adult moth. The rest of the parts make up the abdomen. The abdomen has five pairs of legs, which are called *prolegs*.

Let's Create a Clay Model of a Moth Caterpillar

Learning about the anatomy of a moth caterpillar by creating a model; manipulating materials; following directions
A moth caterpillar has 12 segments in its body and 12 eyes, six on each side of its head! Create a realistic model by shaping modeling clay into 12 balls and sticking them together on a bamboo skewer (Fig. 3-1).

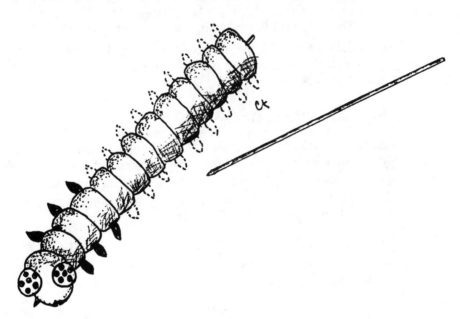

■ **3-I** *A Clay Model of a Moth Caterpillar.*

What you need
☐ Modeling clay or Play-Doh
☐ 6-inch bamboo skewer (You can find these in the cooking supply section of grocery stores or in a kitchen store.)
☐ Styrofoam tray (to use as a work surface and to display the finished caterpillar)

Directions

1. Shape the clay into 12 balls that are 1-inch in diameter. Flatten each ball slightly.

2. Have an adult thread each ball onto the bamboo skewer. To make your caterpillar longer, roll the whole thing gently back and forth with your hands until the segments almost fill the skewer. Add another ball for the caterpillar's head.

3. Make two small circle eyes from the clay and press them on the head. Flatten each eye. A caterpillar actually has twelve eyes! To create these, use another skewer to make six dots in each eye.

4. Model six short legs of clay. Stick one leg on each side of the first three body segments. These are the legs that stay with the caterpillar when it changes to a moth.

5. Create a leaf-chewing mouth by pressing in the clay with your extra skewer. Your caterpillar can be displayed on a Styrofoam tray.

The next stage after the caterpillar is the *pupa*. Many moth caterpillars spin silken cases around themselves. These cases are called *cocoons*. The cocoon protects the pupa from harm while it changes. Many moths do not spin cocoons. The pupa rests in the ground or in rotting wood.

When the time is right, the moth comes out of the cocoon. Some kinds of moths chew their way out and some moths produce a liquid that softens and dissolves the cocoon.

Let's Create the Life Cycle of a Moth

Learning about the life cycle of a moth by creating a model; following directions; manipulating materials; learning to draw with a ruler; using reference material to find out about a moth.
Create four rip-and-tear pictures to show how a tiny egg turns into a moth during a four-stage life cycle (Fig. 3-2).

What you need
☐ 12-x-18-inch sheet of white construction paper
☐ Construction paper scraps
☐ Ruler
☐ Markers or crayons
☐ Glue

Directions

1. Visit your media center and find reference material that describes the moth's life cycle.

2. Fold the sheet of white construction paper in half like a book. Fold it in half again like a hot dog bun. Open it. The creases have divided the paper into four equal rectangles.

3. Use a ruler to draw straight lines on the creases. This step creates four sections. Number each section.

4. Rip and tear paper scraps to create a leaf and a moth egg. Glue them in place in section number one of your construction paper.

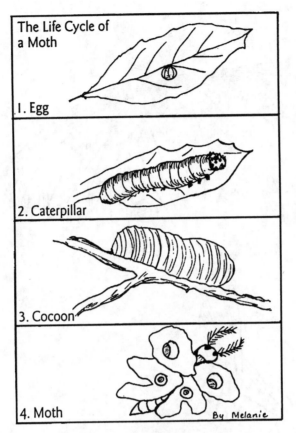

The Life Cycle of a Moth

1. Egg

2. Caterpillar

3. Cocoon

4. Moth

By Melanie

■ **3-2** *The Life Cycle of a Moth.*

5. Rip and tear paper scraps to create a caterpillar in section number two. Draw legs, prolegs, segments, and eyes.

6. Rip and tear paper scraps to create a cocoon in section number three. Draw a branch for the cocoon to rest on.

7. Make a rip-and-tear moth for section number four. Include two antennae, three body parts, and four wings. Glue the parts into place on your construction paper.

8. Label each section of the life cycle. Label the top of the page by writing "The Life Cycle of the Moth."

Adult moths can be less than 1 inch across or as much as 12 inches across. An adult moth has a head, thorax, and abdomen. Its body is covered with scales and hairs. Most moths cannot bite or chew. They use their proboscis (a tube coming from their mouths) to suck up food from flowers. Moths drink water, sip nectar, and drink sap from trees.

Luna Moth

Luna moths (Fig. 3-3) are named for the spots on their bodies. Someone thought these spots looked like moons. *Luna* means moon in Latin. Luna moths have beautiful wings. Their wings extend into long, graceful tails. Some luna moths have green wings, and others have wings that are bright yellow and orange. The caterpillars eat leaves of oak, walnut, hickory, and persimmon trees.

■ **3-3** *A Luna Moth.*

Let's Create a Pocket Puppet Luna Moth

Using reference material; creating a model of a moth; manipulating materials; learning to measure with a ruler

The large green wings of the luna moth are perfect for painting with the soft hues of water colors. Hang the wings on a classroom clothesline to dry. Glue them to a stuffed lunch bag to create a beautiful Luna Moth Puppet (Fig. 3-4).

The paper lunch bag used for this puppet is available in school supply stores in many colors. Although a yellow or green bag would be perfect, plain brown bags work very well, too.

What you need
☐ Paper lunch bag
☐ Newspaper
☐ Stapler
☐ Paper grocery bag
☐ Ruler
☐ White glue
☐ White and yellow construction paper

■ **3-4** *A Pocket Puppet Luna Moth.*

☐ Scissors
☐ Water-color paints and brush
☐ Markers

Directions

1. Find a color picture of a luna moth in your library or media center to use as a guide.

2. To create a realistic model, stuff a lunch bag one-third full of crumpled newspaper. Staple across the bag just behind the stuffing, as shown in Fig. 3-5.

3. Next, create a tail for the moth by overlapping the top of the lunch bag until it forms a cone, as shown in Fig. 3-6. Glue it to make it hold its shape.

4. To make a pocket from a piece of grocery bag, first cut out a rectangle that is 2¾ inches wide and 4¾ inches long. Next, put glue around three edges and stick it to the bottom of the moth body to create a pocket for your hand (Fig. 3-7).

5. Use the patterns in Figs. 3-8, 3-9, and 3-10 to trace two fore wings, two hind wings, and two antennae onto white construction paper. Trace the head onto yellow construction paper. Cut these parts out.

6. Paint both sides of the wings and the antennae with soft greens and yellows to look like a real moth. Hang the wings on a class clothesline to

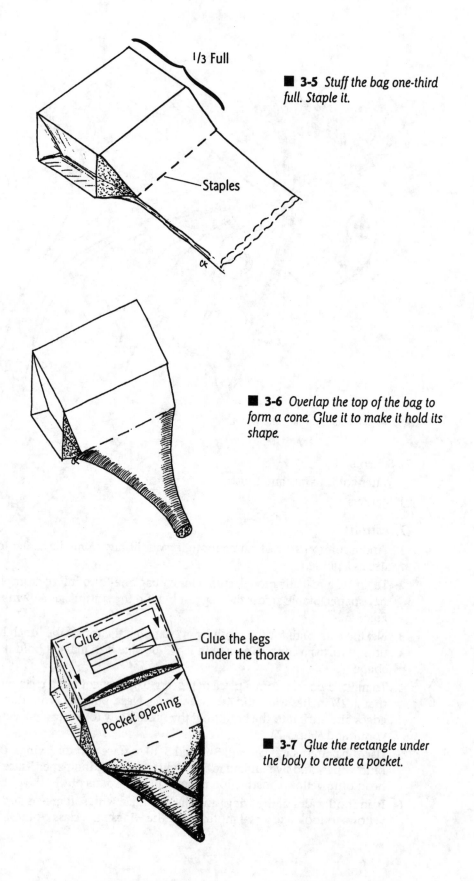

¹/3 Full

■ **3-5** *Stuff the bag one-third full. Staple it.*

Staples

■ **3-6** *Overlap the top of the bag to form a cone. Glue it to make it hold its shape.*

Glue

Glue the legs under the thorax

Pocket opening

■ **3-7** *Glue the rectangle under the body to create a pocket.*

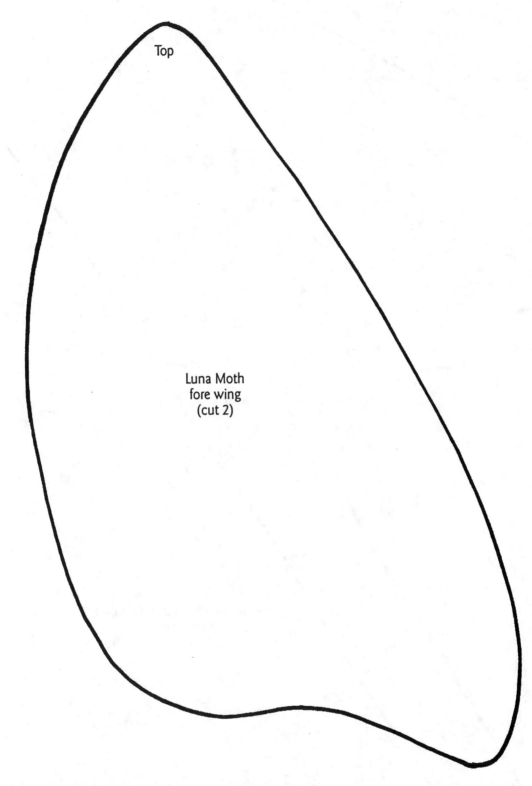

Top

Luna Moth
fore wing
(cut 2)

 3-8 *The pattern for the fore wing of the Luna Moth.*

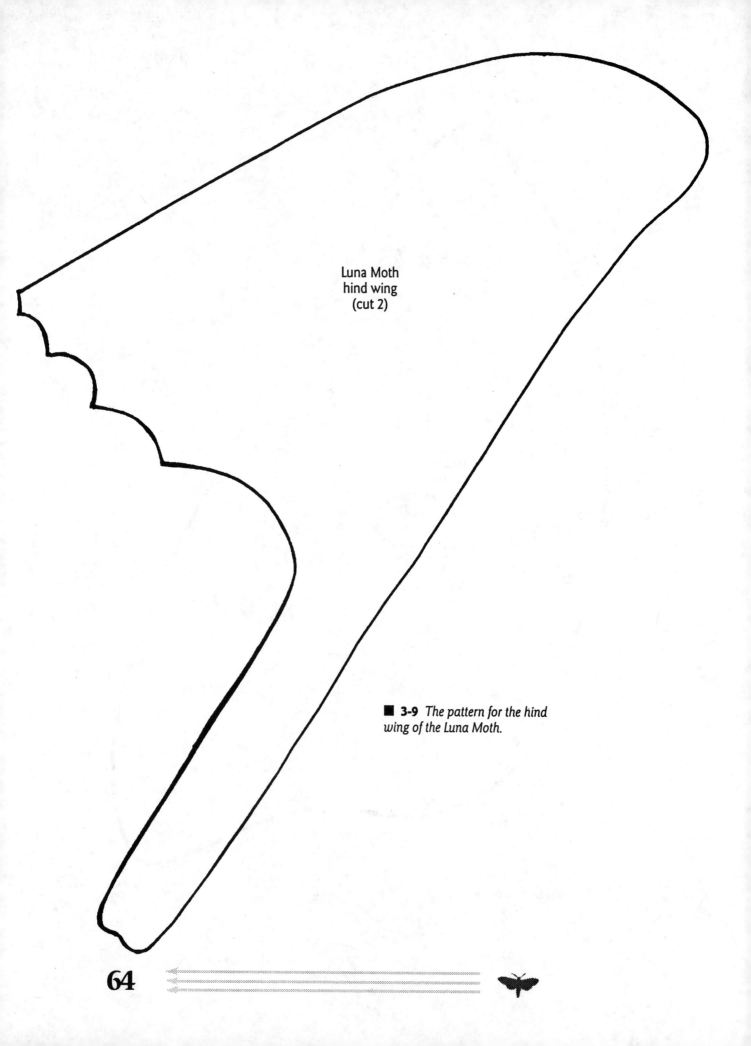

Luna Moth
hind wing
(cut 2)

■ **3-9** *The pattern for the hind wing of the Luna Moth.*

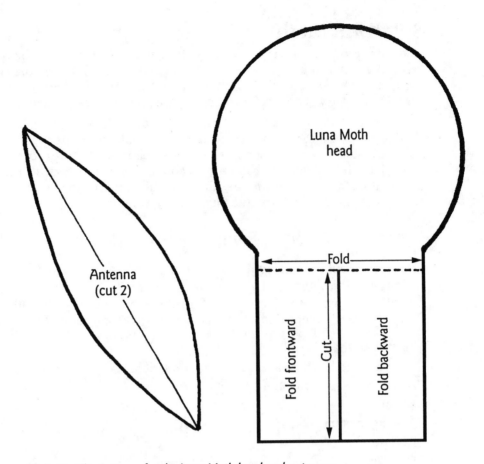

■ **3-10** *The patterns for the Luna Moth head and antennae.*

dry. Then paint brown and black circles on them. Let them dry again. Add yellow veins by drawing on the dry wings with yellow marker.

7. Finish the antennae by adding feathery lines with a black marker. Fringe them with scissors.

8. Glue the hind wings to the top of the thorax, as shown in Fig. 3-4. Then glue on the fore wings. Each fore wing should slightly overlap each hind wing. Lay the luna moth flat with the wings down to dry for 30 minutes or longer.

9. Glue the head onto the front of the body. Glue the antennae on each side of the head. Use markers to add eyes and a mouth.

10. To create legs, cut a 1½-x-7-inch construction paper rectangle. Cut two slits on each side, as shown in Fig. 3-7. Bend the legs and glue them to the underside of the thorax.

Silkworm Moth

Silkworms produce silk. (If possible, provide a piece of silk to show the children.) A mother moth can lay about 400 eggs. In about 20 days, the eggs hatch. The whitish-colored silkworms eat, and eat, and eat. They eat mulberry leaves. The worms can get 70 times bigger than they originally were.

After about a month, the silkworm has become about 3 inches long. It finds a twig and spins a cocoon, which is made of silk. Glands in the mouth give off a fluid that creates fine silk threads. The pupa inside of this cocoon becomes a moth in about three weeks. The moth is white. It is about 1½ inches across. If people want to use the silk from the cocoons, the cocoons are soaked in hot water, and then the threads are unwound.

Let's Create a Pocket Puppet Silkworm Moth

*Observing and recreating a moth; manipulating materials;
following directions*
The silkworm moth is so fuzzy and soft that it seems to be covered with silk itself! Your moth puppet can be covered with wisps of soft cotton (Fig. 3-11).

What you need
☐ Paper lunch bag (Use a white bag if it's available.)
☐ Newspaper to use as stuffing
☐ Stapler
☐ White construction paper
☐ Scissors
☐ Markers
☐ White glue
☐ Cotton balls
☐ Grocery bag

■ **3-11** *A Pocket Puppet Silkworm Moth.*

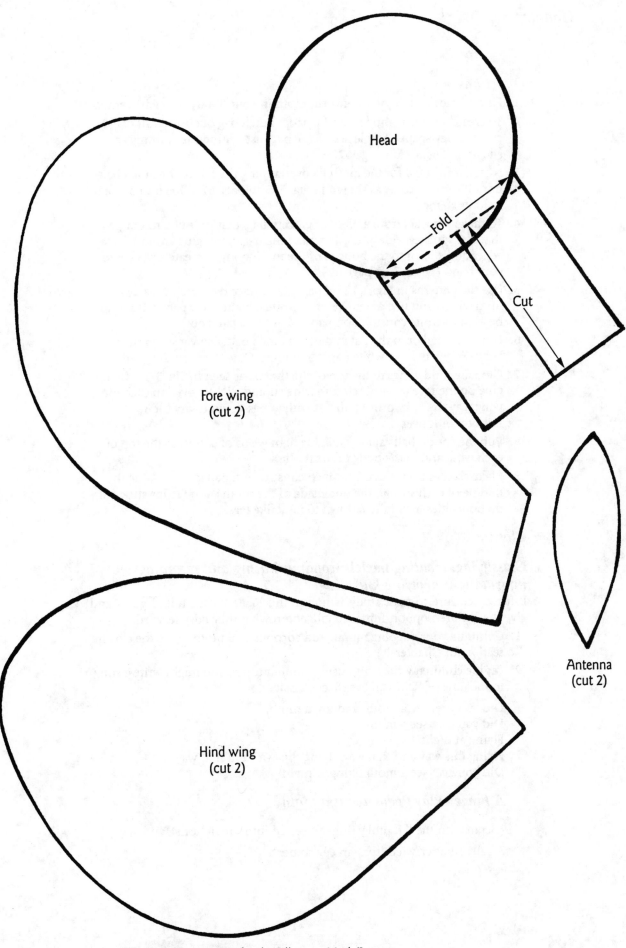

Head

Fold

Cut

Fore wing
(cut 2)

Antenna
(cut 2)

Hind wing
(cut 2)

■ **3-12** *The patterns for the Silkworm Moth Puppet.*

Directions

1. Find a color picture of a silkworm moth in your library or media center.

2. To create a realistic model, stuff a paper lunch bag one-third full of crushed newspaper. Staple across the bag just behind the stuffing, as shown in Fig. 3-5 on page 62.

3. Next, create a tail for the moth by overlapping the top of the lunch bag until it forms a cone, as shown in Fig. 3-6 on page 62. Glue it to make it hold its shape.

4. To make a pocket from a piece of grocery bag, first cut out a rectangle that is 2¾ inches wide and 4¾ inches long. Next, put glue around three edges and stick it to the bottom of the moth body to create a pocket for your hand (Fig. 3-7 on page 62).

5. Use the patterns in Fig. 3-12 on page 67 to trace two fore wings, two hind wings, and two antennae onto white construction paper. Trace the head onto white construction paper. Cut these parts out.

6. Glue the head onto the flat end of the lunch bag. Draw eyes on the head. Fringe the two white paper antennae. Glue them on the head.

7. Glue the hind wings to the top of the thorax, as seen in Fig. 3-11. Then glue on the fore wings. Each fore wing should slightly overlap each hind wing. Lay the Silkworm Moth flat with wings-down to dry for 30 minutes or longer.

8. Pull the cotton balls apart, and glue light wisps of cotton to the top of each wing and to the body of the moth.

9. Make six legs from three 1-×8-inch construction paper strips. Glue the middle of each strip to the underside of the moth so the strips stick out on both sides. Bend them down to look like legs.

☞ Closure

Classifying; creating models; communicating and recording information; applying knowledge

Bringing closure to your study is important. Review your initial goals and give the children opportunities to talk about what they have learned.

1. Continue your ongoing mural. Add cocoons and moths. (See the closure section for Chapter 1.)

2. Let the children write songs using familiar tunes. You might write a song to the tune of "Did You Ever See A Lassie?"

Did you ever see a moth, a moth, a moth,
Did you ever see a moth
Flying at night?
Flying this way and that way, flying this way and that way.
Did you ever see a moth flying at night?

A Finger Play Poem about a Moth

(Begin with the left pinky finger inserted into the right fist.)

A caterpillar crawled from an egg so neat.

(Take pinky finger from fist.)

"I'm hungry," he said. "I want to eat."

(Wiggle the pinky finger.)

He ate some leaves and grew a lot.

(Hold up fingers on the left hand in succession until the thumb is up.)

"I'm tired," he said. "It's time to stop."

(Hold up fat thumb.)

He spun a cocoon and went to sleep.

(Wiggle the left thumb above the left fist, then stick the left
thumb into the left fist.)

All winter long he didn't make a peep.
'Til Spring's warm sun came along and said,
"It's time to get up! Wake up, sleepy head!"

(Say the sun's line loudly! Shake the fist with the thumb inside.)

He got so hot the cocoon he did doff.

(Pull the thumb from the fist. Immediately link it with the right
thumb.)

Then he flew into the night as a beautiful moth!

(Link both thumbs, hold fingers out like wings, and flap fingers to
fly away.)

chapter **4**

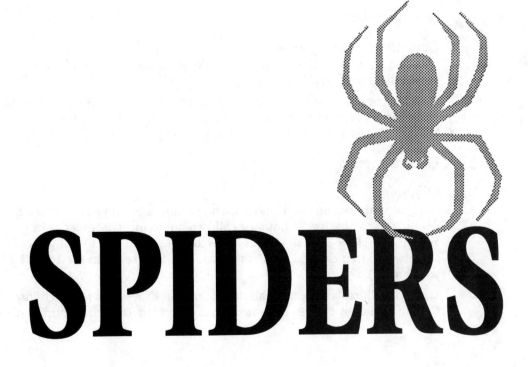

SPIDERS

Science goals

To help children become aware of what spiders are like, how they grow, what they do, and their purpose in the world

Teacher/Parent planning

Borrow informational books from the library. Prepare to write words about spiders on a large sheet of chart paper.

Materials needed for discussion and activities

☐ Informational books
☐ Chart paper
☐ Magnifying glasses

Related words

arachnid Any member of a class of small, land animals that have no wings, four pairs of legs, one to six pairs of simple eyes, no antennae, and two body parts: the *cephalothorax* (head and thorax joined together) and the abdomen.

 "Little Miss Muffet"

 Communicating information

Let the children act out this familiar rhyme:

Little Miss Muffet
Sat on a tuffet
Eating her curds and whey.
Along came a spider who sat down beside her
And frightened Miss Muffet away.

 Fear of spiders

Communicating information

"Why do you think some people are afraid of spiders? Are you afraid of spiders? Why or why not?"

Now is a good time to talk about safety. Some spiders are harmful to people, but most spiders are not. We should not pick up a spider or let it crawl on us. We should quietly move away and let the spider go on its way.

 Let's visit spiders

Observing

Take your children on a walk indoors and outdoors. See if you can find a spider or webs to observe. Remind the children not to touch a spider or its web. You might want to find an abandoned web or a part of one to bring back so that the children can feel it. (Perhaps you can find some in the corners of your house.)

Look for children's videotapes about spiders and show them to the children. Give the children time to look at pictures of spiders in their informational books. After taking your walk and looking at all kinds of spiders in library books, let the children tell you what they think are some characteristics of spiders. Write these descriptions on the chalkboard. After discussion, write the appropriate ones on the chart.

Caterpillar Corner *Many children think that spiders are insects. Be sure, as you move through this study, to help them distinguish between insects and arachnids.*

Spiders are fascinating animals. They are not insects. They have eight legs and insects have six. Insects might have wings and antennae; spiders do not. Spiders are members of a group that scientists call *arachnids*. Spiders, ticks, mites, scorpions, and daddy longlegs are all arachnids. Spiders do not have bones. They have tough skin, which protects their bodies. About 30,000 kinds of spiders live all over the world.

Most spiders are brown, gray, or black. Some spiders are beautifully colored. While some spiders are as small as a dot on paper, others are as big as a dinner plate.

All spiders have special parts of their bodies called *silk glands* that make silk. Some spiders have three silk glands and others have five silk glands. Each gland makes a different kind of silk. Sometimes a spider wants to make silk that is sticky and sometimes it wants to make silk that is not sticky.

Every kind of spider makes a certain kind of silk nest for its home. Some spiders live underwater (like the water spider) and make their nests under the water. Some spiders make their nests under leaves. Some spiders dig burrows under the ground and line the burrow with silk. Other spiders make their nests in their webs.

Wherever a spider goes, it spins a special silk line behind itself. It's like a piece of thread coming from behind the spider, and it is called a *dragline*. If a spider gets frightened, it can fall from its nest or web and still be connected to this special thread. It can hide somewhere and then later climb back up the special thread to return to its nest or web.

All spiders eat other animals. Spiders are very helpful to people because they eat insects that harm farmers' crops and bother people. Some spiders spin webs, and they use their webs to catch their food. All spiders have fangs. They bite insects and other animals, but most spiders are not harmful to people.

Caterpillar Corner *Spiders protect the balance of nature by eating insects. This helps keep the insect population from getting too large. Nature's balance is also protected when spiders are eaten by birds or lizards. The balance of nature is a difficult concept for young children to understand. Explain this concept in an appropriate way for the age of your children. They can start to realize that everything has a purpose and that nature tries to work in harmony.*

A spider begins its life as an egg. Some spiders lay as few as 100 eggs and others lay up to 2,000 eggs. Most mother spiders bundle all of her eggs up into an *egg sac*, which is a silken home that protects them until they hatch. Baby spiders are called *spiderlings*. If the spiderlings are born and the weather is too cold, they stay in the big egg sac until the weather is nice and warm. Then they come out and start to spin draglines. Sometimes the wind makes the spiderling and its dragline float around in the air and the babies travel far away to begin their lives. Spiderlings shed their skin when it gets too tight for their growing bodies, so they get a new, larger skin as they grow.

 Baby spiders

 Creating models
Give each child a small circle (about the size of a dime) of construction paper. Let the children draw a tiny spider on their circle. Tape the end of a piece of sewing thread (about 18 inches) to the back of the circle. Tell the children that this is a baby spider and its dragline. Take the children outside and let them float their spider babies around in the air as they hold the dragline and move about slowly.

A spider's body has two main parts: the head and thorax (joined as one), and the abdomen. A spider's eyes are on top and in front of its head. Different kinds of spiders have different amounts and positions of eyes, but many spiders have eight eyes, two rows of four. Some spiders that live in dark places, such as caves, have no eyes at all.

Spiders are not able to chew. They eat only liquids. The mouth has a part that is like a straw and allows the spider to suck liquids. Near the mouth are the fangs, which spiders use to catch their food.

A spider's eight legs are attached to the head/thorax part of its body. Attached to the abdomen are *spinnerets*, which the spider uses to spin silk. Silk flows through tubes in the spider's body.

A spider has a brain, a stomach, a heart, and lungs. A spider has blood, but the blood has no color.

Garden Spider

 Using reference materials

 Finding information
Help your children look through the informational library books and encyclopedias to find pictures of garden spiders. Talk about what they look like and the kinds of webs they weave.

Garden spiders spin beautiful large webs. They usually spin these webs at night and you might wake up one morning to find a beautiful web on the porch or in your garden. First, the spider spins a line across an open space and secures it to a twig or other surface. The spider adds other lines until it has made a large square or triangle. Next, the spider weaves a wheel with many spokes. Then it weaves circles around and around. It then lays down a sticky silk that traps insects. The spider starts at the outside of the web and works toward the inside. Finally, when it gets to the middle, it weaves a zigzag. This zigzag is interesting to look at, and it lets you know that this is a garden spider's web. The garden spider sits on this zigzag to hide itself from other animals. When an insect is caught in the web, the spider dashes to it and poisons it. The insect becomes the spider's food.

Let's Create an Orange Garden Spider

Observing and recreating a model of an arachnid; using reference material to discover science facts; manipulating materials; following directions; measuring with a ruler

The garden orange spider (Fig. 4-1), or writing spider, doesn't need good eyesight to catch insects. It builds a beautiful web for this purpose, and then "writes" a scribbled message in the middle.

This project can be used to teach measuring as each student measures and cuts out eight rectangle legs.

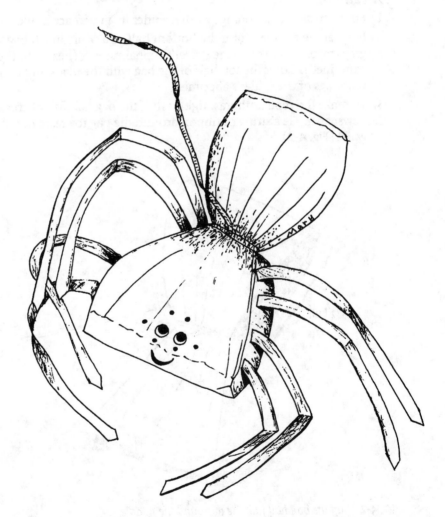

■ **4-1** *An Orange Garden Spider.*

What you need

- ☐ White paper lunch bag or any small white bag
- ☐ Crayons
- ☐ Newspaper for stuffing
- ☐ White glue
- ☐ Yellow and black construction paper
- ☐ Ruler
- ☐ Scissors
- ☐ Paper punch
- ☐ Two small wiggle eyes
- ☐ Ribbon or string

Directions

1. Find a picture of an orange garden spider in a reference book.
2. Look at the picture. Color the bottom half of a white lunch bag with a gray crayon to look like the spider's cephalothorax (head and thorax combined). Color the top half of the bag with the black and orange markings of the spider's abdomen.
3. To make the cephalothorax, tightly stuff the bag half full of crushed newspaper. Tie a string or ribbon around the bag to create the spider's waist (Fig. 4-2).

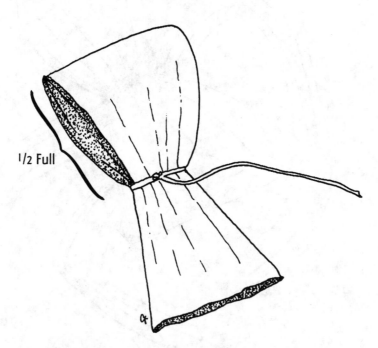

1/2 Full

■ **4-2** *Stuff the bag half full. Tie it around the middle.*

4. Stuff the abdomen with paper. Overlap the top of the bag and glue it closed. Use your fingers to hold the bag closed until the glue begins to dry (Fig. 4-3).

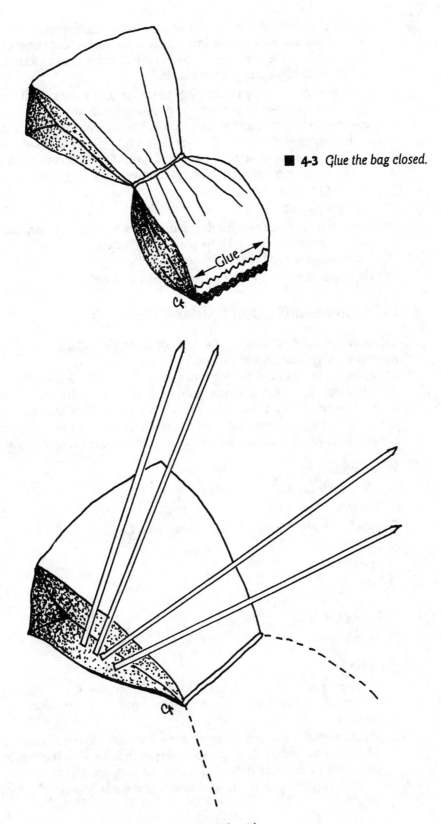

■ **4-3** *Glue the bag closed.*

■ **4-4** *Glue four legs like a fan along the side.*

5. To make spider legs, use a pencil and a ruler to measure and draw eight ½-×-10-inch rectangles on yellow construction paper. Cut them out. Cut one end of each leg into a V-shape to look like the spider's foot. Color the legs with black and orange stripes.

6. As shown in Fig. 4-4, glue four legs like a fan along the side of the cephalothorax. Two legs should be pointing backward a little and two legs should be pointing forward a little. The easy way to do this is to squirt four lines of glue on the side of the spider, and then lay a leg on each glue line. Hold them in place with your fingers. Let them dry for a few minutes before you turn the spider over. Glue four legs in the same way on the other side.

7. After the glue dries, bend down each leg.

8. Glue on two wiggle eyes for the spider's two main eyes. Use black paper and a paper punch to make six paper punch eyes. Glue two eyes above the main eyes, two below, and one on each side.

9. Tie a ribbon to the spider's waist to look like a web.

Let's Create a Garden Spider's Web

Observing and re-creating the web of a garden spider; manipulating materials; following directions

Different spiders build different types of webs. The garden spider creates a beautiful web that begins with a hub, or center. From the hub, it connects thread-like spokes that look like the spokes of a wheel and finishes with sticky connecting strands. You can create a web to hang in the window by sandwiching yarn between sheets of clear contact paper (Fig. 4-5).

What you need

☐ 9-×12-inch sheet of construction paper
☐ Markers
☐ Two 9-×12-inch pieces of clear contact paper
☐ Scissors
☐ Markers
☐ Tape
☐ Yarn
☐ Yellow felt or paper
☐ Paper punch

Directions

1. Observe a real spider web very closely. Notice that it has a hub, spokes that support it by connecting to objects, and sticky connecting strands.

2. On a sheet of construction paper, draw a similar web with a marker. Make your drawing very large and open so that it covers the whole page. Begin with a dot for a hub in the center of the page. Draw the spokes out from the hub (Fig. 4-6). Draw connecting strands between the spokes (Fig 4-5).

■ **4-5** *A Garden Spider's Web.*

3. Peel the paper backing from a sheet of contact paper. Lay the contact paper sticky side up on top of your drawing. You can see the drawing through the clear paper. Tape the drawing and the contact paper to your desk top so they won't move while you're working.

4. Using your drawing as a pattern, lay pieces of yarn on the contact paper to create a web. Start with the hub and spokes, just as you did when you drew the web. Add the connecting strands last.

5. To create a garden spider, use the pattern in Fig. 4-7 to cut a spider shape from yellow felt or yellow paper. Draw a design on the abdomen and draw eyes with a black marker. Stick the spider on the web. Cut eight tiny strips of paper for legs and stick them on the contact paper.

6. Top with a second sheet of clear contact paper, sticky side down. To avoid trapping a big air bubble, begin pressing the two sheets together in the middle of the picture, sandwiching the spider and web in between. Trim the edges of the contact paper with scissors. Punch two holes in the top to thread it with a piece of yarn for hanging, then hang your web in a window.

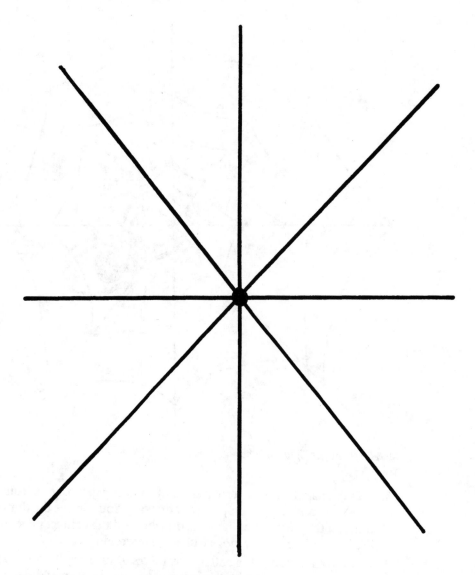

■ **4-6** *The hub and spokes of the Spider Web.*

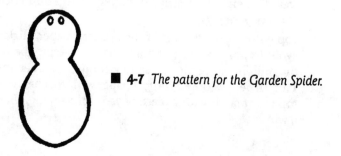

■ **4-7** *The pattern for the Garden Spider.*

Jumping Spider

This spider has excellent eyesight and it catches its food by jumping after it instead of building a web to catch its prey. It has short legs, but it can jump about 40 times the length of its body. This spider can float down after it jumps because it is connected to its own silk thread called a *dragline*.

Let's Create a Pocket Puppet Jumping Spider

Observing and re-creating a model of an arachnid; using reference material to discover science facts; manipulating materials; following directions; measuring with a ruler

The jumping spider has the best eyesight of all the spiders since it must see insects to catch them. It builds a web nest to sleep in at night. You can create your own Jumping Spider Puppet (Fig. 4-8).

This project can be used to teach measuring as each student measures and cuts out eight rectangle legs and a rectangle pocket.

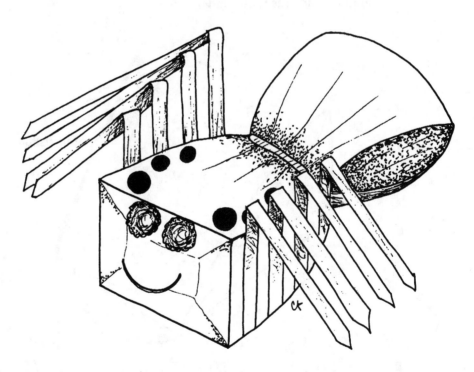

■ **4-8** *A Jumping Spider.*

What you need

☐ Paper lunch bag
☐ Newspaper for stuffing
☐ Stapler
☐ Brown construction paper
☐ Ruler
☐ Scissors
☐ Markers
☐ White glue
☐ Two 1-inch pom-poms or large wiggle eyes
☐ Grocery bag for making a pocket

Directions

1. Find a picture of a jumping spider in a reference book to use as a guide.
2. To make a realistic model, stuff a lunch bag two-thirds full of crushed newspaper. Staple across the bag, about 1-inch from the top. Trim the top of the bag in a rounded shape to look like the abdomen of the jumping spider, as shown in Fig. 4-9.

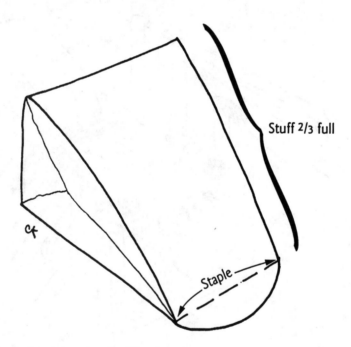

Stuff ⅔ full

Staple

■ **4-9** *Stuff a lunch bag. Staple and trim it.*

3. Create a waist for the spider by tying a string tightly around the middle of the bag, as shown in Fig. 4-10.
4. To make spider legs, use a pencil and a ruler to measure and draw eight ½-×-9-inch rectangles on brown construction paper. Cut them out. Cut one end of each leg into a V-shape to look like the spider's foot.

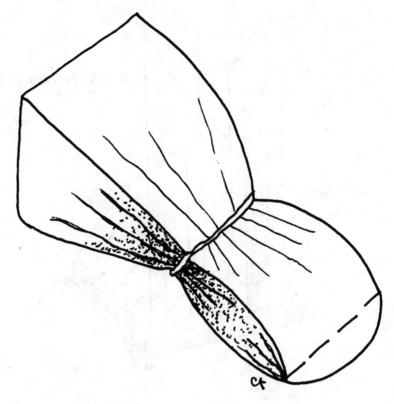

■ **4-10** *Tie a string for the waist.*

5. As shown in Fig. 4-11, glue four of the legs straight up along the side of the spider. (They should look like a fence.) The easy way to do this is to squirt four lines of glue down the side of the spider, and then lay a leg on each glue line. Hold them in place with your fingers. Let them dry for a few minutes before you turn the spider over. Glue four legs in the same way on the other side.

6. After the glue dries, bend down each leg.

7. Glue on two pom-poms (or wiggle eyes) for the spider's two main eyes. With a marker, draw six more eyes on the side of the head, three on each side.

8. Make a pocket for your hand from a piece of grocery bag, as shown in Fig. 4-12. First, cut out a 3-x-4¾-inch rectangle from the bag. Next, put glue around three edges of the rectangle, and stick it to the bottom of the spider's cephalothorax (head and thorax combined). Let the glue dry before inserting your hand.

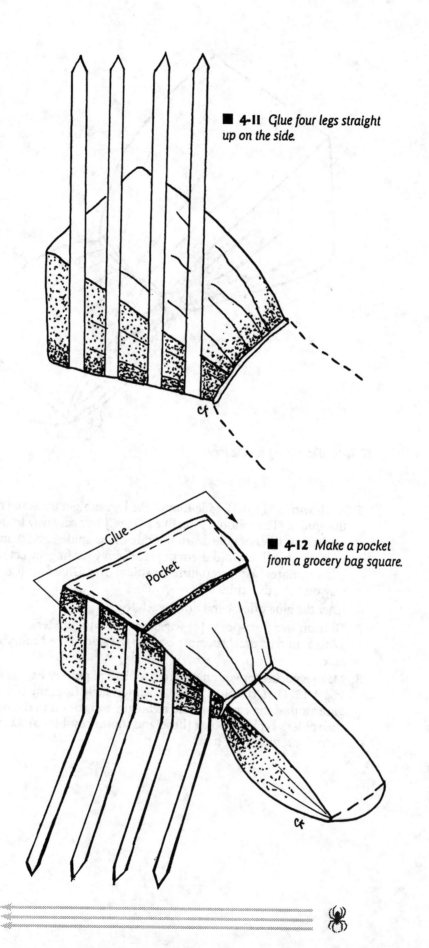

■ **4-11** *Glue four legs straight up on the side.*

■ **4-12** *Make a pocket from a grocery bag square.*

Glue

Pocket

Daddy Longlegs

☞ *Let's find daddy longlegs*

Observing

Take your children for a walk outdoors and look for daddy longlegs. If the children are not familiar with this animal, you can share some of the information below and look at pictures in your informational books. Summer or early fall is a good time to find them. Look on dark, damp walls, under windowsills, near rainspouts, or around plants after a brief rain. Maybe you can catch one and bring it indoors for observation. Hold a plastic or glass jar over or beside it and gently assist it into the jar. Close the jar with a top that allows air to circulate. Plan to set it free in about an hour.

If you want to keep several daddy longlegs for several days, you can use a cardboard box. Put some small holes along all sides. Cover the bottom with plastic and put sand in it. Moisten the sand with water. Put in some stones and twigs. Put a small dish of water in the box too. Put several daddy longlegs in and then cover the top with a piece of clear plastic. You can feed them live insects, bread crumbs, or butter. (They like fat.)

Daddy longlegs are related to spiders, but they are not spiders. They have eight legs like spiders, but they do not spin webs. They belong to a special group of animals called arachnids. Spiders also belong to this family. Daddy longlegs are sometimes called *harvestmen*. They usually do not bite people, and they are not poisonous.

Daddy longlegs come from eggs. When they are born, they look like their parents except they are much smaller. Find a period at the end of a sentence in a book to see what size a baby daddy longlegs would be. As they grow, they shed their skin. They shed their skin five to nine times before they are fully grown.

Daddy longlegs need to live in places where they have a lot of moisture. They stay thirsty. They like cool, shady places. They cannot swim, but they can stand on water and drink. They eat insects.

A daddy longlegs has a small, round body. It doesn't have a neck or waist. It has holes on the sides of its body for breathing. It has two eyes that look sideways. It is not able to blink its eyes. It has a small mouth with two feelers and a pair of pincers, or claws. The claws crush food and put the food in the daddy longleg's mouth.

A daddy longlegs has four pairs of legs. Its legs are covered with little hairs. The second pair of legs are longer than the other pairs. These legs are very important. It uses these legs to touch, hear, taste, and smell. It keeps these legs clean by pulling them through its jaws and then washing its jaws in water. All of the legs are very delicate, so we should be very careful never to pull on any of the legs. Each of the legs has a claw at the end. The daddy longlegs uses the claws to hold on to things as it runs along.

Let's Create a Daddy Longlegs

Observing and re-creating an arachnid; using a ruler;
manipulating materials; following directions

The daddy longlegs, sometimes called a harvestman or a crane fly, is a cousin of the spider. You can create a model daddy longlegs (Fig. 4-13) by adding eight pipe cleaner legs to a gum ball, which is the seed pod from a sweet gum tree.

This project can be used to teach measuring as each student measures and cuts pipe cleaner legs.

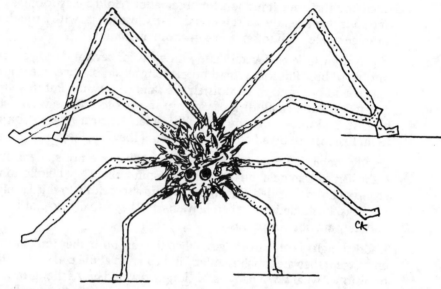

■ **4-I3** *A Daddy Longlegs.*

What you need

☐ A gum ball with a stem, or a 1-inch diameter Styrofoam ball from a craft store, or a 1-inch ball of clay
☐ Scissors
☐ Brown or black pipe cleaners
☐ Ruler
☐ White glue
☐ Paper punch

Directions

1. Measure and cut pipe cleaners into the following lengths:
   • Four 5-inch pipe cleaners
   • Two 4-inch pipe cleaners
   • Two 3-inch pipe cleaners
2. Squeeze a drop of glue onto a scrap of paper. Dip the end of each pipe cleaner into the glue, and insert the pipe cleaners into the gum ball in the following order and positions:
   • two 3-inch legs on opposite sides in the front of the model

- one 5-inch leg behind each 3-inch leg
- one 4-inch leg behind each 5-inch leg
- one 5-inch leg behind each 4-inch leg

3. Finish your model by bending each leg at least once. Glue on eyes made of paper punch circles.

The Value of Cooking with Children

When we cook with children, we introduce them to the wonderful experience of hands-on chemistry and math. As children cook, they gain firsthand knowledge of fractions, the importance of accurate measuring, and the meaning of dry versus liquid measure. They create mixtures and encounter chemical reactions as the individual ingredients change into a totally new substance.

In addition the students have an opportunity to classify ingredients as solids or liquids. (An egg can be both, depending on whether it is cooked or raw.) Older students can list ingredients according to the amount of each in the recipe. This task necessitates measuring, and perhaps weighing, each one to discover "which is more."

 When cooking with children, always consider their safety first. An adult must supervise all cooking activities, making certain that the children are not harmed by hot stoves or sharp utensils.

Let's Create Spider Bread

 Learning about dry measure and liquid measure; using whole numbers and fractions; learning to follow directions
Spider bread (Fig. 4-14) is actually bread that is shaped like a spider! It's easy to make using frozen bread dough.

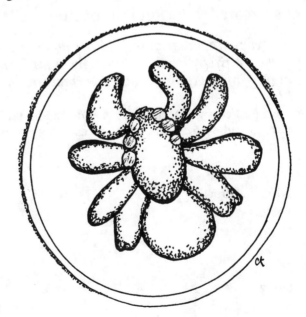

■ **4-14** *Spider Bread.*

What you need

☐ Greased baking sheet
☐ Clean surface for making bread
☐ Half a loaf of frozen bread dough, thawed
☐ Oil for greasing hands
☐ Ruler
☐ Jar with a lid
☐ One egg
☐ 1 tablespoon water

Directions

1. Divide the bread dough into two equal pieces (in half). Set aside one piece for the spider's legs. The remaining piece is the spider's body.
2. Divide the body in half again. Shape one piece into a ball for the spider's cephalothorax. Shape the other piece into a ball for the spider's abdomen. Put them on the greased baking sheet and pinch them together.
3. Divide the remaining dough into eight equal pieces (into eighths). Roll each piece into a leg that is 4 inches long. Use a ruler to measure them. Pinch the legs onto the cephalothorax, putting four legs on each side.
4. Pull a tip off each leg. Stick the tips onto the front of the spider to make eight eyes.
5. Make egg glaze by breaking the egg into a jar and adding 1 tablespoon water. Put the lid on the jar and shake it hard. Brush the glaze all over the Spider Bread.
6. Let the bread rise for 20 minutes. Bake at 400°F for 12 to 15 minutes until golden brown.

Let's Create "A Pocket Full of Bugs" Little Book

Using reference material to find out about a ladybug beetle, a honeybee, a firefly beetle, a butterfly, a moth, and a spider; recording information about these creatures by drawing and writing

Create a pocket page for five insects and a spider until you've made a book (Figs. 4-15 and 4-16). Add a string to each bug so that it can fly and crawl around.

What you need

☐ White construction paper
☐ Scissors
☐ Markers or crayons
☐ White glue
☐ Stapler
☐ String

■ **4-15** *The cover page for "A Pocket Full of Bugs".*

Page 1: The ladybug

Page 2: The honeybee

Page 3: The firefly

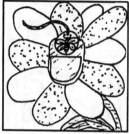
Page 4: The butterfly

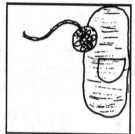
Page 5: The moth

Page 6: The spider

■ **4-16** *Page ideas for "A Pocket Full of Bugs".*

Directions

1. Copy seven pages for the Little Book by using the patterns in Figs. 4-17 through 4-23.
2. Decorate the cover page.
3. Use the pocket pattern in Fig. 4-17 to create six pockets. Glue one pocket on each page. Staple the pages together to make a book.

4. Use the circle pattern in Fig. 4-17 to draw and cut out six circles.

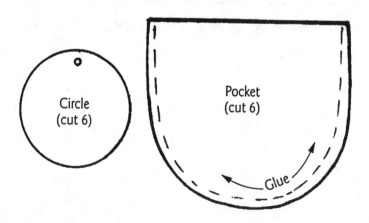

■ **4-17** *"Patterns for "A Pocket Full of Bugs".*

A ladybug beetle _____

_____

Place
pocket
here

■ **4-18** *"A Pocket Full of Bugs" page 1.*

5. Find reference material to help you accurately draw and color the
   following creatures, one per circle:
   • Ladybug beetle
   • Honeybee
   • Firefly
   • Butterfly
   • Moth
   • Spider

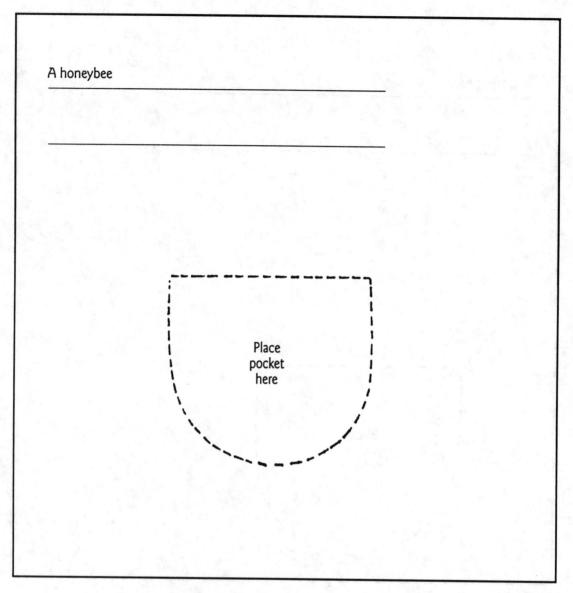

A honeybee

Place
pocket
here

■ **4-19** *"A Pocket Full of Bugs" page 2.*

6. On each page, write one or more facts in sentence form about that insect or spider. Illustrate what you have written by drawing and coloring the book pages as if the pocket were not there. (Fig. 4-16 contains page ideas.)

7. Make a small hole in the top of each circle and tie on a short string (4 inches or 10.5 mm). Insert each creature into its appropriate pocket with the string hanging out. When you read the story, take each one out of its pocket to fly or crawl around on the end of its string.

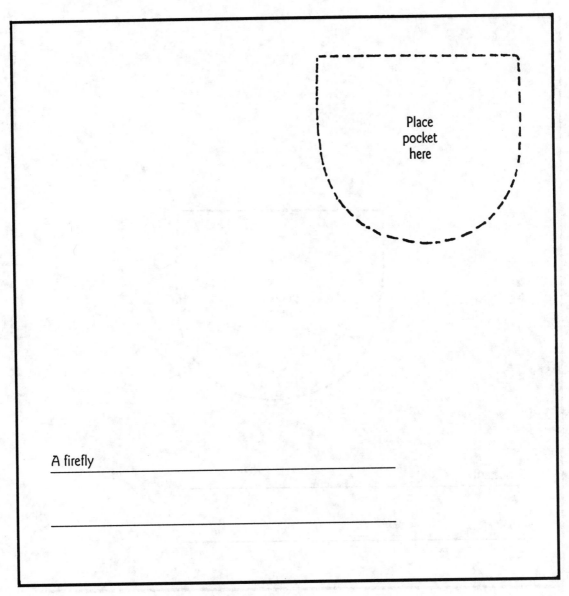

Place
pocket
here

A firefly

■ **4-20** *"A Pocket Full of Bugs" page 3.*

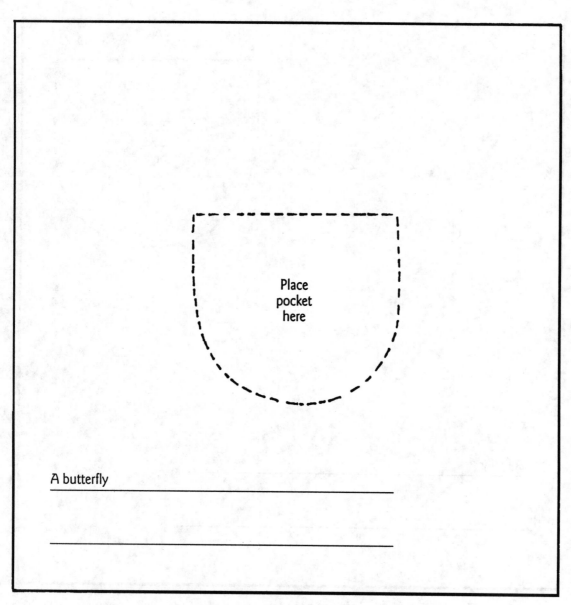

Place
pocket
here

A butterfly

■ **4-21** *"A Pocket Full of Bugs" page 4.*

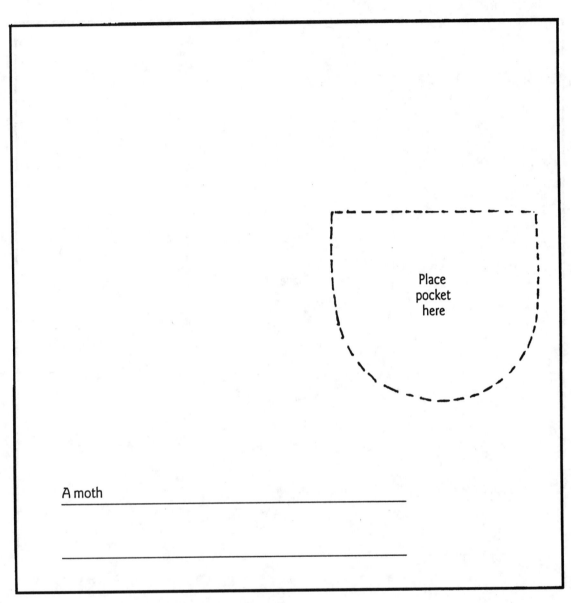

Place
pocket
here

A moth _____

_____

■ **4-22** *"A Pocket Full of Bugs" page 5.*

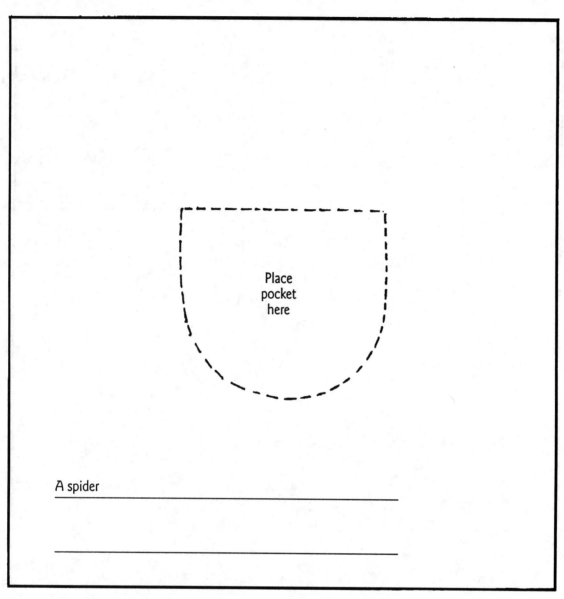

Place
pocket
here

A spider

■ **4-23** *"A Pocket Full of Bugs" page 6.*

Let's Create a Bug-O-Rama

Creating a model of an environment where one might find various insects and spiders; follow directions; manipulate materials; learn about solid and liquid measurement

Making a bug-o-rama (Fig. 4-24) can be fun! First you make your own clay with flour and salt. Then create a scene on wood and add plastic models of insects and spiders.

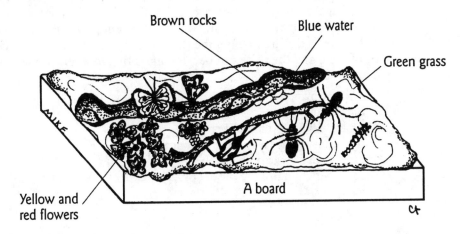

■ **4-24** *Bug-O-Rama.*

What you need
- ☐ 4 cups flour
- ☐ 1 cup salt
- ☐ 1½ cups water
- ☐ Large bowl
- ☐ Red, blue, green, and yellow liquid food color
- ☐ Board (can be scrap plywood 6 inches square)
- ☐ Small rocks and twigs
- ☐ Plastic models of insects and spiders (Available in school supply stores.)

Directions
1. Measure the flour, salt, and water into a bowl. Mix it into a dough. Divide the dough into four pieces. Make a hole and squirt a different food color in each piece of dough. Squeeze the dough to spread the color.
2. Spread green clay all over the top of the board. Add blue clay for water, red clay for rocks, yellow clay flowers, or anything else you can imagine.
3. Stick on small rocks and twigs. Add plastic insect and spider models in areas where you think they might live.
4. Write a story about life on your Bug-O-Rama.

Closure

Asking Questions; finding Information, communicating information

Bringing closure to your study is important. Review your initial goals and give the children opportunities to talk about what they have learned.

1. Continue to add to your ongoing mural. The children can add spiders, spiderlings, and daddy longlegs.

2. Use the spider models the children created earlier. Act out "Little Miss Muffet" again, but do it a new way. Substitute any child's name and let each child decide what he or she wants to be eating. (Let them really be eating.) Instead of frightening the child, the spider should tell the child about itself, and the child can be a loving, caring listener. The poem might go like this:

Little Mr. Brown
Sat on his chair
Eating his peanut butter and crackers.
Along came a spider who sat down beside him
And told him how to spin a web.
(Let another child use the model of a spider to talk to Mr. Brown.)

or

Little Miss Jane
Sat on the rug
Eating her ripe, red apple.
Along came a daddy longlegs who sat down beside her
And said, "Can you help me find a nice, cool place to rest?"

Index